THURSDAYS WITH EUGENE

THURSDAYS WITH EUGENE

A MEMOIR OF LIVING WHILE YOU THINK YOU'RE DYING

BY DONNA R. DINKIN

NEW DEGREE PRESS
COPYRIGHT © 2022 BY DONNA R. DINKIN
All rights reserved.

THURSDAYS WITH EUGENE
A Memoir of Living While You Think You're Dying

ISBN   979-8-88926-408-8   *Paperback*
             979-8-88926-409-5   *Digital Ebook*

Dedications

For Joseph, Noah, and Sylvester

Contents

THE PITY PARTY	9
AUTHOR'S NOTE	11

PART 1. — 17

ACCEPTING THE NOW: LAUNDRY DAY		19
CHAPTER 1.	THE DIAGNOSIS	23
CHAPTER 2.	EUGENE	33
CHAPTER 3.	I CAN'T HANDLE THE TRUTH	41
CHAPTER 4.	CATASTROPHIZING	51
CHAPTER 5.	THE ME BEFORE	61
CHAPTER 6.	THE MONSTER: ANXIETY	71

PART 2. — 79

ACCEPTING THE NOW: WORK TRIP		81
CHAPTER 7.	HOW ARE YOU?	85
CHAPTER 8.	AM I IN THE FIGHT?	95
CHAPTER 9.	CONTROLLING THE UNCONTROLLABLE	103
CHAPTER 10.	I'M PISSED AT YOU	111
CHAPTER 11.	THE GLASS IS HALF FULL	119
CHAPTER 12.	DO YOU HAVE ANY QUESTIONS FOR ME?	129
CHAPTER 13.	BEN & JERRY'S	141
CHAPTER 14.	TIME WELL SPENT	151
CHAPTER 15.	THE IMAGINARY TOOLBOX	161

PART 3. — 173

ACCEPTING THE NOW: BEDTIME RITUALS	175

CHAPTER 16. OXYGEN DROP	179
CHAPTER 17. THE RESILIENCE TEST: COVID-19	189
CHAPTER 18. ART AND THE ROSEATE SPOONBILL	199
CHAPTER 19. NEXT THURSDAY	211
ACKNOWLEDGMENTS	215
APPENDIX	223

The Pity Party

I'm having a party
And you are invited

There is music and dancing
Food, drinks, and party favors
The room is decorated in brightly colored streamers
And a disco ball is spinning from the ceiling

I'm having a party
Right now, inside my head

There is crying and sadness in the corners
Regrets and worries float by in a parade
Anger and pain sing loudly for all to hear

Join me at my pity party
And please
Don't forget to bring your dancing shoes

Donna R. Dinkin, 2019

Author's Note

I'm not sure what road I thought I would be on at age sixty-ish, but the road to Duke Medical Center was not in my top ten guesses.

If I had asked my thirty-five-year-old self where I would be in twenty-five years, I might have guessed that I would be driving from Noordhoek to Hout Bay on Chapmans Peak Drive in South Africa or weaving my way through crowds on Lan Kwai Fong in Hong Kong. Instead, I spend a good deal of time on the road to the hospital for assessments and tests to manage my health.

That's because in fall 2015, I was diagnosed with pulmonary fibrosis or lung disease caused by the autoimmune disease scleroderma.

This book chronicles my journey to emotional wellness. This journey was not about curing or improving my physical health. That's not possible with my illnesses—not yet, anyway. This journey is about the work I had to do to accept this new and unexpected adventure and to become emotionally stronger. First, I wanted to get through the panic I felt after being diagnosed, but as time went on, I also wanted to build the skills and attitude necessary to handle whatever else life puts in front of me.

The sometimes crippling response I had to my diagnoses is common. People who receive bad news are likely to experience a variety of emotions like fear, sadness, anxiety, depression, and denial. These unsettling moods and feelings can lead to poor compliance with medical treatment as well as added, but avoidable, personal suffering.

Despite these facts, many health care professionals do not receive training on how to deal with the emotional side of chronic illness, and therefore rarely refer patients or their family members to mental health experts as part of their medical care plan.

I was fortunate. I was able to find a guide who helped me build acceptance and resiliency. Over the course of four years, I met with a Gestalt-trained therapist named Eugene. Through our work, I learned that caring for my mental well-being was as essential as taking care of my physical health.

Friends told me about Eugene. Several years prior to my medical diagnoses, these friends spoke highly of his ability to help them through various challenges. I credit him with my growth, although he would say I did the work. (Actually, he would say, "You can't speak for me. You don't know what I would say.")

I've always wanted to write a book but didn't think I had the talent. Writing was always my go-to answer whenever anyone asked, "If you had the ability to do anything, what would you do?" Someone with musical talent might say, "I'd play the cello like Yo-Yo Ma," while another person who has an entrepreneurial spirit might answer, "I'd be like Bill Gates."

Writing is something I always wished I had the talent to do. I suppose I could have written a work-related book either on public health leadership or organizational crisis preparedness, areas I studied for years. But if I could have been anything, it would have been a writer of people's stories. Over the years, however, I had enough self-doubt in my abilities that writing a creative memoir never made it on my to-do list.

The thought of writing this book emerged as I read the stories of others who had experienced similar life-threatening health events. I found books about dying or facing death oddly comforting. I could relate in a different way to the stories these authors shared. I was scared with them, I laughed with them, and I was frustrated with them. In their books, I highlighted text that resonated with me and wrote notes about my own stories in the page margins as I read.

Nina Riggs, for example, wrote in her book *The Bright Hour*, "Is it fucked up that I keep buying clothes for the kids when they're much older? Yesterday, I went to the Gap outlet near the cancer center and spent a fortune on twelves and fourteens in boy's pants. And, I've been browsing prom dresses" (2017, 263).

I also recall thinking that I needed to do a lifetime of "mom things" before time ran out, such as making plans for my son to get his license when he was still years away from being able to take the driver's education class. While some might say these kinds of books are depressing, I found them cathartic. They felt like a support group or special club, and these thoughts made me feel less alone.

To gain control of the chaos I felt after being diagnosed, I kept notes. I recorded all of my symptoms and complaints in an Excel spreadsheet and updated it every other month. I made lists of questions, recorded test results, and jotted down tidbits from meetings with doctors in notebooks. I used a thick, leather journal that was given to me as a gift by a team of nurses I once worked with, capturing my emotional struggles and the highlights from conversations with Eugene.

The times I felt numb, frightened, confused, angry, grateful, and happy can be found scribbled in the pages of the documents I kept. Through these notes, I started to realize how important my emotional health was to my sense of peace and happiness, regardless of the status of my physical health. I relied on these notes to share my story.

In December 2020, I read Lori Gottlieb's book *Maybe You Should Talk to Someone*. Her story of working on a challenge with a therapist inspired me to write my own story about how Eugene helped me learn to be curious about what is and to be content with how I choose to spend my time.

To some, this all may seem like a winding road of self-pity, negativity, grief, and messiness—and it is. I accept that those feelings are part of being human. The joy for me, and hopefully for you, is in seeing that I have come to accept and celebrate those emotions but also not dwell on them.

Scleroderma and pulmonary fibrosis are progressive diseases. Aging is relentless, too—no turning back. These conditions will present many challenges along the way. I suspect that I will react to new issues related to my diseases or to my aging body by screaming, crying, and being negative. That's okay with me. Because of my work with Eugene, I will also laugh, love, and enjoy what is in front of me.

I hope that by sharing my story I'll provide support to others who are facing existential confusion and anxiety after experiencing a life-altering event. I hope it inspires members of the medical system to do more to care for the emotional side of a person while they treat the physical side. Finally, I hope that my story will serve as a catalyst for academic leaders teaching the next generation of health and mental health providers to bridge the divide in care. After all, humans are not split into sides and pieces. Our physical health affects our emotional health and our emotions affect our physical health.

Eugene once told me, "Sometimes people who say that they want a good cry just want a good ramble." I hope my rambling feels like hand-holding to someone having a good cry.

PART I

Accepting the Now: Laundry Day

Today is a laundry day.

The washer and dryer are in the mud room, which is located between the garage and the kitchen. The bed sheets and dirty clothes from the week are piled high on the floor of the bathroom right off the master bedroom. That room is on the second floor of the house.

To get to the second floor, I must walk up the staircase in the middle of the house, a total of fifteen steps. I take this walk at least once per day at bedtime, but it's not uncommon for me to make the climb more often. Since I didn't kick the laundry down the stairs this morning when I made my way to the kitchen for coffee, I will need to walk up the stairs to get the laundry I want to wash today.

If I wasn't obsessed with my lung function levels and breathing abilities, I might forget that I had any diseases for the first eight steps. I climb these steps with ease and without thought. However, on the ninth step, I suddenly hit a wall. My legs feel it first. They feel the same level of fatigue as if I ran a half-marathon. The slippers on my feet are suddenly Frankenstein's boots, too heavy to lift. My heartbeat intensifies; I can hear it. It pounds in my throat, beating faster. My chest has tightened and my rib cage is as heavy as a bag of cement.

By the time I get to the landing on the second floor, I wonder if I was holding my breath while walking up the steps. I don't actually remember breathing. My body tells me to stop moving. I'm hungry for oxygen; the air I am taking in is unsatisfying. Perhaps this is what it would be like to try to breathe in space. My lungs aren't helping. I envision them as small balloons located at the base of my throat, next to my heart, unable to hold air. In an attempt to get more oxygen, my breathing becomes more rapid and shallow. It does not, however, improve my situation.

As I try to satisfy my oxygen need, I find that the air I am taking in is irritating my already-inflamed trachea. Breathing is like rubbing lotion on sunburned skin. I start coughing, which makes it even more difficult to breathe. I have learned that one cannot breathe and cough at the same time. I strongly urge myself to relax. If I'm successful, the coughing will lessen.

After fifteen seconds of standing on the landing to the second floor of my home, my legs are starting to feel lighter, my breathing and heart rate begin to slow, and my coughing subsides. My heart seems to move from the base of my throat back to its place in my chest. I cautiously take the first three to four steps into the master bedroom and find I can resume walking at a normal pace.

I see the pile of laundry on the floor in the bathroom and think, *I'll get to it later.*

CHAPTER 1.

The Diagnosis

Six years before my trip to get laundry, I sat on the second to bottom stair on this same staircase in the foyer of my home. The sun shined through the large palladium window above the front door and hit me as I sat. The warm sunlight streaming through the window was why the staircase was our dog's favorite place to sit each afternoon. It may have been a lovely day and the dog may have been lying in his usual spot, but honestly, I don't recall. My eyes were open but I was blind to everything around me. I didn't move, or maybe I couldn't move. My head felt empty and full at the same time. I knew I was in trouble.

After a minute or thirty minutes—it's hard to know—I called my husband at his office and told him I'd just heard from the doctor's office. Without a thought as to whether or not I was interrupting his work, I blurted out, "They want me to come in to see the doctor tomorrow. They have the results of my tests."

An appointment had already been scheduled for the next week, but the nurse who called me was certain that the doctor wanted to see me the next day rather than wait the additional days. It must be really, really bad, I concluded. On the call, my husband said that he would go with me to the appointment. He probably even tried to reassure me that everything would be alright. I don't remember.

I didn't maintain the healthiest lifestyle throughout my life, but when asked to fill out forms in a doctor's office, I typically checked the box that said I was in excellent health. But was I?

As an adult, my choices regarding diet, exercise, and general well-being would not have earned me any special awards. While I studied public health nutrition in graduate school, I drove to the neighborhood Burger King every night for a burger and fries. My peers ate granola and raw veggies. My true academic interest was in global malnutrition although I lacked the maturity at the time to see how my fast-food diet was probably contributing to my own poor nutritional status. Despite my academic training, I never really turned my eating habits around. I will, however, hide spinach in my spaghetti sauce or homemade soups.

In my forties, I took up jogging with some friends and ran a few races with them over the years, including my second half-marathon two weeks shy of my fiftieth birthday. We called our running group The Muffin Tops. This name accurately describes my physical appearance now but was a joke at the time we were routinely running. My running pace was a ten-minute mile, which wasn't fast enough to win any races but was enough to pat myself on the back for the effort. My race participation medals hang on the cork board in my home office and serve as reminders of the joys of friendship and good health.

My fiftieth year, 2011, was difficult. My husband and I had been struggling and decided that we needed to separate. I was also working on an intense project with an unrealistic timeline and menopause had just come knocking on my door. It was a perfect storm. At this time, my heart started flipping around inside my chest. I believed the sudden irregularities were due to all of the stressors in my life and the fact that I was keeping myself going with continuous refills of caffeinated coffee. After seven to ten days of heart palpitations and shaky hands and legs, I considered going to a doctor. In a week, I was scheduled to travel to Rwanda and Tanzania for my work project and I thought that it would be wise to check out my heart before such a big trip. As it turns out, while the coffee may not have helped, the real issue with my heart and my limbs was a malfunctioning thyroid gland. The night before I left for Africa, four years before I found myself sitting on the steps in my foyer, I was told that I have Graves' disease.

Graves' disease, I learned, is an autoimmune disorder that targets the thyroid gland—a gland that sits at the lower front of your neck. It produces hormones that regulate the body's metabolism as well as other functions. With Graves' disease the thyroid gland over-produces thyroid hormones, a state known as hyperthyroidism, causing a variety of symptoms including anxiety, irritability, hand tremors, weight changes, bulging eyes, and heart palpitations. I was given Valium for possible anxiety and then left for Rwanda the next day.

My trip to Africa went off without a hitch and I returned to Washington DC to finish the final report for my project. Two months later, I started treatment.

The doctor recommended the most common form of treatment: radioactive iodine therapy (RAI). I was told that when the radioactive isotope (I-131) is taken orally by a patient, the radiation that is attached to the iodine is absorbed out of the blood into the thyroid gland. Over a few months it destroys the overactive cells. On August 22, 2011, I swallowed a horse pill of radioactive iodine, and by late fall my thyroid was considered dead. At this time, I was given a prescription for a daily hormone replacement pill.

Since I did not exercise while I was receiving treatment, it was not surprising that I felt out of shape when I eventually tried to jog or ride a stationary bike. All of my muscle memory from the years of jogging and exercising seemed to be gone. I decided to commit to a regular training schedule using my stationary bike to rebuild my strength. Unfortunately, it soon became apparent that despite my effort, I didn't get stronger; in fact, I could barely add any tire resistance at all during my rides. After just a couple of minutes of spinning my foot pedals, my muscles yelled for me to stop and I was out of breath. I whispered what I had so many times before: "You're lazy."

By 2013, my husband and I had reconnected and our family of four was together again under the same roof. That summer, we all went to Europe and I learned that my youngest child had inherited some of my wanderlust, or was at least willing to be my travel buddy if I paid for everything. In spring 2014, he and I planned a trip to Peru to see Machu Picchu, the ruins of an ancient Incan citadel, located in the Andes Mountains near the city of Cusco. One must travel to an altitude of eleven thousand feet above sea level to reach this area.

While preparing for our trip, I learned that high altitudes can cause some people to get sick. Since I seemed to be running out of breath more easily, I began to wonder if I would have problems with breathing in the mountains. At a regularly scheduled doctor visit to test my blood thyroid hormone levels, I asked about this concern. As a result, the doctor did a chest X-ray. From this, he told me that I have asthma and recommended that I see an allergist for treatment when I returned from my trip. Unfortunately, we never tested my breathing abilities in Peru. We had to cancel the trip because my son got sick the day before our adventure was to start.

I was comfortable with the asthma diagnosis. Asthma was common and, in my mind, not anything to worry about. I told myself that a runny nose, wrinkles, and asthma were just the kind of things that happened to aging women. Six months later, I returned for a follow-up visit with the allergist. My symptoms had not improved so she had me do another breathing test and then prescribed an inhaler. Meanwhile the doctor who was following my thyroid hormone levels suggested I take a calcium channel blocker for what I had self-diagnosed as a new case of Raynaud's syndrome.

Raynaud's syndrome causes small blood vessels in various parts of the body, often the hands, feet, and nose, to constrict in response to cool temperatures or stress. These areas turn colors such as white, blue, or purple as oxygen is limited by the narrowed blood vessels. Raynaud's can also cause numbness or stinging pain, and in severe cases it can lead to sores or gangrene. My mother had Raynaud's for a while, so it was not a surprise when I started being annoyed by similar symptoms in the middle of the hot North Carolina summer months when air-conditioning often runs at full blast. My mom used to say "cold hands, warm heart." In my case, the cold hands turned out to be a missed red flag.

By the end of the summer in 2015, I was fortunate to travel to South Africa for another team project. The project required us to interview government officials throughout the country. The office buildings we visited rarely had elevators. We typically had to walk up flights of steps to get to our meetings.

One interview with a very senior health official took place on the third floor of an old but beautiful governmental building. The staircase was wide and spiraled as each curve ascended to the next landing. The stone steps were worn in various places and uneven in height. As I struggled to climb up, it hit me that something was not right. I was trying to pass as healthy, stopping as if nothing was wrong and waiting for others in our work group to catch up. By the time we reached the third floor, my days of believing I had a "touch" of asthma were over.

I'm not sure what I thought was wrong, but I know I didn't envision anything catastrophic. Maybe I was just so out of shape I couldn't walk up steps? I was overweight and I was getting older, almost fifty-five years old at the time. Or perhaps my thyroid hormone levels were off and this was making me breathless. Whatever the reason for my difficulties, what I told myself was, *you're a lazy, fat hypochondriac!*

Just days after my return home from South Africa, my follow-up visit with the allergist ended with a referral to a lung specialist.

During the ten days before my scheduled appointment with "Dr. Lung," as I'll call him, I convinced myself that the visit was not necessary. I wouldn't cancel the appointment, but afterward, I'd be sure to have my thyroid hormone levels checked and ask for my medicine dosage to be adjusted.

When I saw Dr. Lung on September 25, 2015, he didn't object to me having my thyroid hormone levels tested, but he advised me that it would also be prudent, given my symptoms, to schedule some additional tests. He ordered a Computed Tomography or CT chest scan, blood tests, a pulmonary function test, and an overnight oxygen test. This seemed like overkill in my humble opinion. But, dutiful patient that I am, I complied. My follow-up appointment was scheduled for Friday, two weeks later.

Just one week later, however, I found myself sitting on the second to bottom step of the staircase in the foyer of my house, staring into space after having received a surprise phone call from a nurse in Dr. Lung's office. Doctors only have one reason for wanting you to come in the next day instead of the following week: you'll be dead by then. At least, that is what I told myself.

My overactive imagination suddenly viewed Dr. Lung as the Grim Reaper. The next day, as I entered the medical building for my appointment with him, plaintive sounds of Albinoni's Adagio in G minor for cellos blasted through my brain.

Dr. Lung's feet shuffled in the hallway outside the exam room. My husband and I looked nervously at each other when he tapped on the door and entered. "Hello, Ms. Dinkin," he greeted us, washing his hands and grabbing the black stool from the side of the room to sit beside us. Sensing our anxiousness, he jumped right in with the news we were there to learn.

"The CT scan shows no evidence of blood clots in your lungs" he said, scanning from my eyes to my husband's as he prepared to deliver the diagnosis, "but it does show some inflammation, which is consistent with something called interstitial lung disease."

I stared at him, trying to make sense of his words. Inflammation? Disease? Lung? The words replayed in my head.

Dr. Lung explained that my blood tests and my history of Graves' disease, as well as the presence of Raynaud's syndrome, suggested that the lung disease was caused by the rare autoimmune disease scleroderma. It seemed I was one in thirty million.

"I'm going to send you to a rheumatologist for their opinion," he said.

Though my body stayed upright in my seat, inside I collapsed. A wave of mental noise flooded me.

I had never heard of interstitial lung disease but I could not imagine that anything labeled as lung disease would be minor. Unfortunately, I had heard of scleroderma.

In the late 1990s, I watched a movie called *For Hope* (1996) that documented comedian Bob Saget's sister's experience and death from a debilitating disease: scleroderma. I was always interested in movies or shows about medical mysteries. To this day, I watch the TV show *Medical Diagnosis* with the expectation that I will determine the cause of the illness before the show's narrator shares it. While watching the docudrama about Bob's sister, I recall being horrified by her experience. What I remembered years later was an image of a woman who rapidly turned to stone and died.

When Dr. Lung suggested my lung disease might be caused by scleroderma, I went blank. I heard almost nothing else from my conversation with him except for the question my husband asked at the end of our visit: "Why was it important that Donna be seen today rather than at her scheduled appointment next week?" Dr. Lung said that another patient had cancelled and since my test results were in, it made sense to see me sooner. I heard his words, but really, I heard him say, "because she is dying."

CHAPTER 2.

Eugene

I could hear and feel someone telling me I was dying.

They were urging me to hurry and make all the decisions I needed to make but hadn't yet. They were telling me to buy a red sports car so one of my boys will be happy when I leave it to him in my will. They were telling me to clean up the attic so I don't leave it for others to clean. They were telling me to make the baby book for my youngest son that had been on my to-do list for years and to take a trip with my sister before it was too late to do so.

Intellectually, I was aware that these thoughts were coming from myself alone, but I nevertheless felt powerless to stop them. Years would pass before I understood that my body was generating these thoughts as it attempted to digest all of the incoming data about my life and the world around me. Eventually, I learned that I needed to welcome my inner voice's comments and let them go, again and again, until they didn't return. In the meantime, however, I blamed all of these intrusive thoughts on some otherworldly being: my mind!

It didn't take me long to recognize that I needed help taming my unwanted thoughts. While brochures and support groups may be helpful for some, I needed some one-on-one hand-holding. Within five days of my diagnosis of lung disease by Dr. Lung, I found myself sitting in Eugene's office. At least two of my friends had mentioned him to me in the past. Fortunately, his name was unique enough that it had stuck with me. I had no problem finding him and his therapy practice when I searched for him online. Other than his reputation for being helpful, however, I didn't know much about him. Quite frankly, it didn't matter.

Therapeutic counseling was not new to me. My mother took my brother, sister, and me with her to see Dr. Mind, a therapist in our town, after her separation from our dad. My sister was having outbursts at home and I surmised that we were asked to attend the therapy sessions with Dr. Mind to fix her. I was about fourteen years old at the time, my sister was about thirteen, and my brother nine. All I recall from these sessions was Dr. Mind pointing out that each of us was responding to our parent's separation in different ways. Somehow, we turned the feedback into nicknames. I was Rose, the "perfect" child. My sister was Victim, my brother was Baby, and my mother was Guilty. If my mother was alive today, she would agree that the names still fit almost fifty years later, although me being called "perfect" would be a joke now. I'm not sure the therapy helped us much, but eventually, we grew up and managed to successfully coexist with four hundred to six hundred miles between us.

When my youngest son was diagnosed with a medical issue as a toddler and when my marriage was imploding several years later, I also sought professional help. While I thought

I benefited from my visits with therapists over the years, I later realized that most of my interactions with them were spent rambling, complaining, and blaming others. I'm not sure this approach led to all that much growth. Perhaps I wasn't very open to growing.

Walking into Eugene's office that first time, I was unaware that my work with him was going to be different—very different.

Eugene's office was on the second floor of a two-story building located on a main road that cut through the city, adjacent to an old historic neighborhood. While the building that Eugene worked in was boxy like an office building, it had an old home feel when you walked in through the front door.

Eugene worked in a psychotherapy practice with three other colleagues. They shared a small waiting room, which was located next to Eugene's office. The furniture in the waiting room was old and worn. An oversized, rust-colored sofa was pushed against a wall. The cushions had lost their shape after years of visits from people in search of help. The room had a small table and a set of Lincoln Logs in a basket on the floor for children, and attached to the wall at one end of the room was a bulletin board and shelf with resource materials. A few vintage playbills and concert posters were framed and displayed on the walls. A door to a bathroom was sandwiched between the massive sofa and a Queen Anne wingback chair.

Eugene's personal office space was plain, more of a small room than an office, really. He met patients in this room, but I saw no indication that he did much of anything else there. Two timeworn sofas were placed opposite one another, against opposing walls. At the far end of the room sat a wooden rocking chair with an old brown cushion tied to the seat and within reach of several tissue boxes scattered on the floor. A small desk with a phone and a few scattered papers on top was pushed along the wall across from the office door. The room was so small that the end of the desk almost touched the sofa on that wall.

Eugene's office did not offer any clues about him or his capabilities. He had no personal items anywhere in the office. No diplomas or other wall hangings were mounted on any of the walls, nor were there any family pictures on the desk. He also had no books, art pieces, or trinkets from trips abroad displayed anywhere. The office space felt bare. I trusted that my friends had vetted his abilities, plus I was in crisis. I didn't have time to question whether Eugene's interior design abilities were a reflection of his counseling abilities.

My initial therapy goal was to reduce the panic I felt as well as the suffering I was experiencing from high levels of anxiety. I didn't know what healing would look like; I just needed the craziness in my head to stop. Thankfully, Eugene didn't run away when I walked through his office door for the first time. He walked toward me. We met weekly at first and then every other week for a little over four years.

The type of therapy that Eugene practiced, he told me, is called Gestalt. As I came to understand, he believed that individuals should focus on the present—the "now"—and should take ownership of their thoughts and actions. At the time that I walked into his office, however, the type of therapy he practiced didn't matter to me. I just wanted help.

Soon, I started to understand.

Eugene and I had two conversations early on that gave me insights into his style of therapy. The first occurred after I said to him, "My mind is causing me a lot of suffering." He jumped in before I could explain.

"There's no such thing as a mind," he said with conviction. "What is a mind? It's not like, after you die, they pull out an organ and say, 'Oh, here's her mind.'"

He continued as I scribbled his comments in the writing journal I brought to each session. He believed that people use the concept of a mind as a crutch, saying things like, "My mind made me do it," or "My mind told me."

His statements were interesting and I didn't disagree. In my journal, however, I wrote "Eugene focuses a lot on the words that you use. That's frustrating." Later, I would learn that his focus on words had to do with his belief that I needed to take ownership of what I was doing to myself.

I also started to realize that his approach to therapy was different than my previous experiences when I said during another visit, "I can't breathe. I'm dying."

He responded by saying, "Are you having trouble breathing now? Are you dying right now?"

"Well, no. Not right now," I replied, wondering why he was asking me these questions. *Is he being sarcastic or is he really concerned?*

"What is happening right now?" he then asked.

"I'm sitting here talking to you."

"And how are you experiencing your body, right now?" he said again, emphasizing the words *right now*.

I decided to just follow his lead and continued answering. "Um, I feel good. I feel like I am breathing normally."

"Feel?" he questioned my use of that word, making the point that I was creating thoughts, not feelings.

"Okay, um . . ." I thought for a minute and then said, "I'm breathing normally."

"How are you doing now?" he asked. I was beginning to see his point.

"I feel better—less worried," I answered, recognizing that I actually felt somewhat lighter.

Whereas some people get stuck in the past, I tended to get stuck in fictional futures. The question "Is it happening to you right now?" forced me to focus on the "present" rather than the tragedy and melodrama I imagined.

As our relationship progressed, Eugene became more aware of my tendencies until one day he said, "Donna, you are very creative. You are always writing a book, but it's always a murder mystery."

He was right. I would come to accept that I fabricate narratives, but at the time of my diagnoses, I felt that my "mind" had me trapped in a nightmare and I was banging at the door for someone to let me out.

CHAPTER 3.

I Can't Handle the Truth

What do you do between the first doctor appointment, where you hear "You are dying," and the next doctor appointment, where it will be confirmed that you are dying? You go on living, of course. You make lunch for your children, you do laundry, you pay your bills, and you finish your work projects. I'm sure I did all of this, but I don't really remember. I was in a fugue, not of the musical kind but of the psychiatric variety. I had to keep moving ahead with the events scheduled in my paper calendar, my treasured (if old-fashioned) method of keeping track of plans. Eventually, I asked myself, how does one live while they are dying? But at this point, I wondered: How do I live for the next few weeks?

During the month between the appointment with my pulmonologist, Dr. Lung, and the next specialist, Dr. Rheumatology, I walked around in a stupor, moving but not able to see anything beyond six inches in front of me. But I was a mom with kids at home and a team member on projects at work. The world kept turning and I was powerless to stop it. I had to keep going and pretend everything was okay. Well, I didn't have to, but that's what I did. Actually, I deserve an Academy Award for my performance. I kept going.

My youngest son was in high school and I had to attend soccer games, parent-teacher conferences, and meetings about student field trips. I had a few business-related excursions planned, including trips to Boston and Chicago, as well as a number of additional in-person and online meetings. Hoping to disprove my health concerns, I also made time for some exercise throughout this month. Sure, it would be awkward, but it would also be a relief to say at my forthcoming doctor's appointment, "I'm fine. I was just lazy and out of shape. There's really no need for you to see me." Unfortunately, my attempts to cycle on my stationary bike and to jog in the neighborhood proved the opposite. I was still short of breath upon exertion and my legs felt too heavy to move.

Despite my observable busyness, if I had to tell someone how I spent my time during the month of October 2015, I would say I spent my time in my head, most often creating horror stories. I was so consumed with trying to make sense of what I was going through that I was unable to pay attention to anything else. I don't recall Abby Wambach retiring from soccer at this time, nor do I remember the significant earthquake in Pakistan or the Democrat or Republican presidential candidate debates (actually, I may just be blocking this one out of my head intentionally). Life was a blur, as if I was driving from point A to point B and not remembering the drive.

Around this time, I recall going out to dinner with a friend to a tapas restaurant. I said to her as we waited for a pitcher of sangria to be brought to our table, "The weird thing is, other things no longer matter to me. I am only thinking about myself and what's important to me."

Her response caught me off guard. She said, "I envy your ability to focus on only things that matter."

The word envy stuck out to me. "You envy me?" *Who envies a sick person?* my inner voice questioned.

She continued, "My life is so chaotic. If I could just focus on myself, I would do what I really want to do."

"Which is?" I begged her to continue.

"I'd quit my job and open my own office," she said quickly, making it clear she had been thinking about this for some time.

I agreed that gaining focus was a gift, but in my head, I said, "Yeah, the ability to focus on only one thing would be enviable if the thing you were focused on was not *death*." My friend gained focus a few months later and quit her job. I take some credit for her courageous act.

As my meeting with Dr. Rheumatology approached, I drafted a list of questions to be asked in the notebook I kept to record my own health-related events. Information about my pregnancies, the travel vaccines I have received, and my gall bladder surgery were all recorded in the notebook. My desire to log such events was inspired by my mother's due diligence in keeping track of my health as a child. When I went away to college, she gave me a two-and-a-half-inch by four-inch Health and Immunization Record that she had been maintaining. In the pages of this small book, she had briefly recorded my medical history: chicken pox on

November 12, 1962; broken collar bone on November 8, 1967; Sabin vaccines on multiple dates; a fractured right wrist on July 30, 1975. This record was taped to the back of the adult size notebook that I now kept.

I flipped to a new page in the notebook and wrote at the top the doctor's name, the date, a space holder for my weight and blood pressure readings, and then my list of questions:

Do I have ILD (Interstitial lung disease) or scleroderma? (Spoiler alert—I have both!)
Was this caused by my radiation treatment?
Do I have cancer?
Do I have pulmonary hypertension?
Do I need a lung transplant?
What is my prognosis or life expectancy?
What are my treatment options?

I was pleasantly surprised to be immediately called back into the clinic when I arrived at Dr. Rheumatology's office on November 19, 2015. On that first visit, I don't believe that I even sat in the waiting area. This efficiency was remarkably different from the long and boring wait times I endured at my follow-up appointments with the doctor I saw for my thyroid issues. Dr. Rheumatology appeared to run a tight ship, and for some reason this offered me some measure of comfort. I needed someone that was competent and ready to solve my problems. Dr. Elmer Fudd need not apply.

Dr. Rheumatology's practice was new, so the layout and interior design of her office space was modern and clean. The exam room they placed me in was small but large enough to fit multiple people. I sat on a bench that was part of a desk-bench unit attached to one wall in the room. The nursing assistant entered the room and took my temperature and blood pressure. She then confirmed the accuracy of the medicine list she saw in my electronic medical record: ibuprofen as needed and daily levothyroxine, my thyroid replacement hormone. As I recall, the assistant said nothing that would comfort me or that would let me know I was in good hands. I later concluded, through what felt like thousands of doctor appointments, that my interactions with the people who weighed me, took my vital signs, and checked my list of medicines always felt robotic.

Following the exit of the nursing assistant, Dr. Rheumatology entered the exam room. She warmly greeted me, sat on the rolling stool which brought her to my eye level, and asked, "What brings you here today?" This question seems to help the provider assess how steep of a climb they have for helping the patient understand what is going on with their health. I rattled off my medical history over the last few years, including my most recent visit to the referring physician, my new pulmonologist. I spoke like I was a colleague, very matter of fact, in an effort to hold back a wave of nausea and a total body collapse.

As soon as I was done talking, she got straight to the point.

"Developing Raynaud's syndrome late in life is a red flag. This should have triggered some investigation into autoimmune problems," she began.

It suddenly became clear to me that this red flag had been missed over a year ago by Dr. Thyroid, or as I now thought of him, Dr. I Missed the Warning Signs. Dr. Lung saw it. The blood tests he ordered a month ago highlighted the possibility of scleroderma. Dr. Rheumatologist was ready to confirm this diagnosis and the dire outlook.

I took notes as she talked, but since I was unfamiliar with most of her words, my notes consisted of sentence fragments and partial words. "Vasculitis test was normal, muscle test, normal, sarcoid something? Probably not that, shogren (which is actually, Sjogren's Syndrome) test was normal. My CL70 (which is actually SCL70, an antibody considered to be specific to scleroderma) was positive."

What I clearly captured was her statement, "There are treatments to help with symptoms, but there are no treatments to cure or change the progression of this condition."

The doctor spent an ample amount of time with me and, similar to all of my doctors following her, wouldn't answer the question about how long I had left to live. At the end of our visit, I understood four things:

1. The ILD was likely caused by scleroderma (SSc).
2. The immunosuppressant drug Cellcept (mycophenolate mofetil) was the preferred method of treatment.
3. I needed to be monitored for pulmonary hypertension.
4. The Arthritis Foundation would be my best source of information.

I left the exam room with a brochure in hand and tears welling up in my eyes. I was so distraught that I couldn't exit the building after my appointment for ten to fifteen minutes. I spent most of this time standing alone in front of a wall display of health brochures, staring blindly ahead in shock. I used my sleeve to wipe away the tears that trickled down my cheek from my right eye.

Like most people over age fifty, I had already experienced other difficult situations, two of them related to the health of my sons. Both had experienced health concerns early in life, and in each instance, I handled the situation like a desperate mom on a mission. Recovering from shock after a few days of hearing their concerns, I pressed into action to learn more, searching for information, scouring the Internet, joining online parent support groups, and connecting with experts wherever I could find them. I was not shy about researching academic journal articles on their issues to find the most knowledgeable scientists and emailing or calling them directly for advice. I'm not sure if this would happen today, but not one professional I cold called ignored my plea for information. Both my sons are healthy now.

My approach to dealing with my own diagnosis was different. I wasn't curious to learn about my illnesses. The reality of what I was being told was too frightening. I simply couldn't handle the truth.

As time went on, I did make an effort to understand more about my diagnoses. However, in the early days, I didn't have much luck absorbing new information. A few minutes of online searching shut me down. Fear of the truth is a power force. One night—the worst time to do research—I was sitting in bed and decided to search for articles that would answer my most pressing question at the time: *How much time do I have to live?* Searching the Internet using the words *scleroderma, interstitial lung disease,* and *prognosis,* I found an article that had been published just two months before my diagnosis. In short, it confirmed my fear that the life expectancy of people with scleroderma and lung disease is reduced. The median survival of these patients was between five to eight years (Yasuoka 2015, 97-110).

If I had been reading a real book at the time, I would have slammed it shut. With frightening speed my heartbeat quickened, my throat tightened, and my breathing became rapid and shallow. I started to run the numbers in my head. I'm fifty-four now; I'll be fifty-nine in five years. My children will be in their early twenties. Will they be out of college? Unwanted scary images started to form in my head. *Dying at fifty-nine is bad enough,* I thought, *but what if ages fifty-four to fifty-nine are actually a living hell?* Needless to say, I didn't sleep well that night or any of the other nights I attempted to learn more about my situation. The old adage, "knowledge is power" felt true when my children were ill. It couldn't have felt further from the truth for my own health issues.

Even though it took some time and there were several starts and stops, I eventually felt more at ease discovering what was happening to my body. Ultimately, I learned that scleroderma is a rare disease in which the skin or other connective tissues of a person's body become hard and tight. The symptoms of scleroderma vary greatly for each person and the seriousness of the disease depends on the parts of the body which are affected.

My official diagnosis is "limited systemic sclerosis (SSc) complicated by interstitial lung disease." This means that the buildup of scar tissue (fibrosis) is primarily occurring in some of my internal organs, like my lungs, gastrointestinal tract, blood vessels, and to a lesser extent my skin, mostly in my fingers.

Interstitial lung disease (ILD) is a group of chronic lung disorders distinguished by inflammation and scarring that make it hard for the lungs to get enough oxygen. When ILD is chronic, it is often called pulmonary fibrosis (PF).

Pulmonary fibrosis is a restrictive lung disease as opposed to an obstructive lung disease, like COPD, chronic obstructive pulmonary disease. People with obstructive lung diseases have difficulty exhaling the air in their lungs. People with a restrictive lung disease have trouble fully expanding their lungs with air. The sensation of restrictive lung disease is similar to the feeling one might have if a belt was tightened around their chest, limiting expansion. Personally, I prefer to envision a reticulated python or boa constrictor wrapped around me rather than a Gucci diamond belt. I view myself more like Crocodile Dundee than Paris Hilton.

I recall saying to my doctor a few months after my diagnoses, "These are not good diseases to have."

He responded by saying, "Donna, there are no good diseases to have."

True! But in my head, I said, *These suck.*

CHAPTER 4.

Catastrophizing

"If I have a piece of broccoli between my teeth, keep it to yourself. I can't take any more fuckin' bad news," I yelled out loud in the car as I drove myself to what felt like the two-thousandth medical test in two months, an echocardiogram.

Thankfully, the echocardiogram is a relatively easy medical test. It doesn't hurt and it is done quickly. It's an early, non-invasive procedure that is used in the process of identifying a serious condition called pulmonary hypertension (PAH). The test had been ordered to rule out PAH.

I really didn't know anything about pulmonary hypertension but had heard of it before. Dr. Lung and Dr. Rheumatology mentioned that it was of significant concern to someone with my conditions. In addition, my roommate from freshman year of college had died from PAH, amping up my concern. This was just another thing I added to my growing list of worries.

The path to uncovering the ways in which one's illness impacts their body can be a long, taxing journey—at least, it often is for those with scleroderma. The clues started popping up after my treatment for Graves' disease, but once I was officially diagnosed, I had to check every body system to see where and how this disease was showing up. I knew it was affecting my lungs, my extremities, and my gut. Checking the status of the blood vessels between my heart and lungs, as well as the status of my right heart ventricle, was next. My head was spinning trying to understand why yellow caution lights were flashing all over my body.

As I drove the twenty minutes from my home to the heart clinic for the echocardiogram, I felt exhaustion from all of the tests and troubling thoughts I was generating. Just then, my cell phone rang. Later when my sons began driving, I nagged them about the dangers of talking on the phone while driving. But here I was, rummaging through my purse to find the phone, trying to avoid hitting the car in front of me as it slowed for the red light ahead. Since I had not programmed the number into my contact list, I knew the call was not a friend. Against my better judgment, I answered.

"Hello?" I said, combining the greeting with the question, *Who is this?*

"This is Marsha, calling from the breast imaging center about the mammogram you had yesterday."

After it was clear that I knew who she was, she continued. "There is an area on one of your breasts that we would like to look at further. We've scheduled you another appointment on Monday."

After politely ending the call, I screamed, "What the hell?" This was the last straw—or was it the straw that broke the camel's back? Whatever it was, I couldn't take any more bad news. Not. One. More. Thing. If I wasn't already running short on time for my heart test, I would have pulled my car over to sob.

Arriving at the heart center, I took the elevator up to the third floor. This was a familiar place. I had been to this clinic when I had my thyroid problem a few years back. At that time, the doctor gave me a monitor to wear to confirm my assertion that my heart was flipping out.

My comfort with the building didn't help me on this day. I sat down and surveyed the sterile waiting room. I was the youngest visitor, so I thought. I've since recognized that while I may feel young, I'm old. Perhaps I was just as old as all of the other patients and family members seated in the area, but at the time, I questioned what such a young person was doing in a place like this.

The technician called my name and I followed her through a maze of exam rooms. She was practically sprinting, seemingly unaware that her heart patients might not be able to keep up.

Once in the exam room, I followed her instructions to remove my blouse, put on a robe, and lie on a bed. After dimming the lights, she squirted cold gel on my chest and guided a handheld wand in the area of my heart. I could hear a clicking sound as she recorded different measurements on a computer screen, which was placed next to the bed. If the outcomes weren't so important, the test would actually have been relaxing. But on this day, I was scared to death. *Will the fast heart rate that I'm experiencing now make me fail the test?* I wondered.

To prevent me from jumping off the table in a panic attack, I decided to imagine myself supporting my mom through the procedure. If she were the patient, I would have said, "Oh Mom, it's nothing. It's almost like a massage. It will only take fifteen minutes and the worse part will be rubbing the goo off of your boob with the flimsy gown that they gave you to wear." Since this time, I have found this activity of pretending to help others to be a helpful strategy for getting through medical tests.

Ignoring the advice that Eugene had given me—to be present and smell the roses (my words, not his)—I drove home on autopilot. Then I waited for the results.

That weekend, I found the courage to search Dr. Google for information on pulmonary hypertension. The Mayo Clinic describes it as "a type of high blood pressure that affects the arteries in the lungs and right side of the heart" (2022). Of the seven signs and symptoms listed on the Mayo Clinic's webpage, I was only experiencing shortness of breath. I was not dizzy or having fainting spells. Nor was I experiencing blue lips, chest pain, or swelling ankles. Even though I didn't have most of the symptoms, however, I convinced myself that if the doctor thought a heart test was necessary, I must have PAH. I imagined the artery connecting my heart and lungs exploding at any moment. The ticking stopwatch from the TV news show *60 Minutes* played faintly in the background.

As my anxiety grew, I listed the questions I wanted answered in my personal medical notebook:

How long before I'm totally disabled?
Is this my last Christmas?
How can I prevent losing our house from the costs we'll incur from my illness?
Do I need to move closer to a big medical center?
What do I do with the time I have left?
What is my legacy?

The next time I saw Eugene, I told him how I had added suffering to my plate by researching pulmonary hypertension. "The activity made me spiral into an uncontrollable bout of anxiety," I rambled on.

"The activity did not do that," he said. "*You* did that."

The comment jolted me out of my "woe is me" sulking. I tried to understand the point he was making but struggled. I considered his comment. "I understand that I was the one to look up the information," I said, trying to clarify my point, "but it was the information that gave me the anxiety."

"No. The information does not have the power to give you anxiety."

My eyes glazed over as I tried to process what he was saying. He continued, "You attached judgment and emotion to that information. If I asked you to find information on another medical condition, let's say, prostate cancer, would you react the same way?"

That question piqued my interest. Recently, my friend's husband underwent prostate cancer treatment. I was concerned and saddened but not riddled with anxiety. I felt sure, however, that I would be more anxious if it were happening to my own husband.

As if he were reading my mind, Eugene leaned forward in his chair and asked, "What benefit are you getting from catastrophizing?"

I really didn't know, but I felt his stare so I said the first thing that popped into my head. "It helps me not ignore things that might be important."

"It?" he asked as if he were reprimanding a child.

Annoyed, I thought, *Come on! You know what I'm talking about. Why are you picking apart my words? Does it matter that I said "it?"*

Then I said, "Catastrophizing. Catastrophizing helps me not ignore things that might be important."

It took a long time for me to understand why Eugene was so focused on the language I used. Often, he stopped me mid-sentence if I used certain words. I kept a running list of them in my journal. The list included:

It
Try
Should
Wish, want
Mind

But
Shame, guilt
Better, bad, good—any judgment word

I came to learn that Eugene viewed language as an important indicator of how one positioned themselves in a situation. Pointing out the words I used helped me take ownership of what I was doing to myself. They aren't doing it to me. It wasn't doing it to me. My mother and father weren't doing it to me. I needed to accept that the world was doing what it does and I was the one making meaning of what was in front of me. During the first several months after my diagnoses, the meaning I derived from the breast exams on top of all of the other exams was equivalent to "apocalypse."

Eugene gave me homework. Select a date, time, and agenda for a Meeting to Worry (MTW). The MTW would be a time when I could really focus on my catastrophizing, if that's what I chose to do. I have come to appreciate this exercise because it allows me to be who I am—a catastrophizer—but to also move on after I verbally vomit all the things I've collected to worry about.

Sunday at noon, I met with myself at my office desk and decided it was time to worry (not that I had been all that good at resisting it before that time). Pen and pencil in hand, I decided my top agenda item for the meeting would be the question, *How would I find joy if I became bedridden?*

Before you judge my topic for this meeting, know that I responded to my medical diagnoses and my new life activities—such as dealing with doctor appointments, medical tests, and health insurance—with fear. Being afraid can rearrange the topics on your to-do list. Being afraid can also make you generate weird or unthinkable thoughts. Eugene would probably say, "You have thoughts and then you apply scary feelings to them." That is what I did. I applied scary feelings to all of my thoughts.

On my first MTW meeting, I generated a list of activities I could do if I was unable to get out of bed but still wanted to have fun. The list came in handy during the COVID-19 lockdowns. It really wasn't so outlandish after all.

- Create family scrapbooks
- Watch old movies
- Do jigsaw puzzles
- Write a book
- Interview people over the phone or do research
- Create a new product
- Play cards or online games
- Laugh and visit with friends
- Read
- Draw, paint, or sculpt

On the following Monday in early December 2015, after the echocardiogram and my visit with Eugene, I went back to the breast imaging center for a higher-level mammogram and was told to come back the next day for a biopsy. I was starting to feel numb. I made a mental note to add *What if I have breast cancer?* to my next Meeting to Worry agenda. I just couldn't handle it on that day.

The day of the biopsy, I checked in and took a seat in the waiting room. After a few minutes of waiting, a nurse called me into the clinic. We exchanged our typical American "how are you" greetings.

"I had a rough morning. The lid to my coffee was not on the cup properly and some of it spilled as I was driving," the nurse complained in response to my greeting.

"Oh yeah, my morning has been equally rough. I'm trying to figure out how to deal with diagnoses of scleroderma, interstitial lung disease, and possible pulmonary hypertension. And now I'm here so you all can tell me whether I also have breast cancer. Fuck your hard morning!"

I didn't say it. But I thought it. Fortunately, she didn't say any more and I was able to pass as a sane adult.

My non-response to the brief conversation with the nurse as we walked to the procedure room exploded inward instead of outward. I swallowed my anger and wondered if it was too much to ask health providers to recognize that no one is visiting them because they are having a good day. How could they be so clueless about the situations that brought us there as patients that they'd complain about something so petty? Had this clinic employee welcomed me by saying, "Welcome Donna. My day is fine and I'm happy to be able to help you. You're in good hands. Let me escort you to the clinic," what a difference it would have made for me.

By the end of the week, I learned that all of the tests showed that I didn't have pulmonary hypertension or breast cancer. Of course, I convinced myself it was only a matter of time until I did.

CHAPTER 5.

The Me Before

———

I read obituaries. I started slowly, now and again reading the few paragraphs that family members had written about a loved one's entire life. My interest in obituaries grew after I had to consider what to say about my parents when they passed. Some obituaries are short and sweet and others include information about careers, family members, hobbies, adventures, and crises.

I always believed that my family history and childhood experiences were boring, rather vanilla and generic. Even though my path hasn't been as exciting as those of Oprah, Malala, Tom Hanks, or Bill Gates, obituaries have taught me that everyone has a story to tell and that mine is just as interesting.

My mother's side of the family are Mayflower descendants. My eleventh great-grandfather, William Brewster, arrived with the rest of the ship's passengers to what is now known as Plymouth, Massachusetts. He became an elder and leader of the community, but by the time my mother was born three hundred and fourteen years later, her family struggled with poverty. She wrote in a memory book she made for me, "My memories of my childhood home are not good. There were big rats in the cellar and sometimes we had no heat, food, or clothes." By her early twenties, to escape the burden of being the primary breadwinner for her mom and four siblings, she married her first boyfriend: my dad.

My father was the oldest child of a family whose origins are known only as far back as the migration of my great-grandparents from Belarus and Ukraine at the turn of the twentieth century. He never spoke of his childhood or his family. When I asked him for my Bubba's (grandmother's) special Matzo ball soup recipe or for any other information on the Dinkin ancestry, he sent me to ask one of his sisters or his brother.

After a brief courtship in 1957, my parents drove from their homes on the north shore of Massachusetts to Seabrook, New Hampshire to elope. In response to the question in the memory book, "What was your wedding day like?" my mother shared, "We had enough money to get a motel room for the night, a bottle of soda, and a bag of chips." They returned to their separate homes until the secret marriage was revealed a few weeks later during an argument between my mother and grandmother.

Neither family was fond of my parents' partnership. My mother once told me that her mother didn't like my dad's personality. "He's brash and full of himself," she shared, repeating what her mom, my grandmother, had said. She also believed that she was not liked by my dad's parents because she was not Jewish. She was a non-practicing Protestant and my dad became a non-practicing Jew over time. For a few years while growing up, we attended Sunday school at the temple in the next town, but we never had a bar/bat mitzvah. We celebrated Christmas, Hanukkah, Easter, and Passover. My siblings and I tended to most enjoy the holidays that included gifts and imaginary characters.

We stood out in our small town of 16,000 people and in our neighborhood of about forty homes. I don't recall any comments about us being Jewish, though we were definitely in the minority, but my dad stood out because he brazenly wore red shoes, sported a handlebar mustache, and drove a little sports car.

"What's up with your dad? He's wearing girls' shoes!" a kid said, taunting me one day as he ran through a neighbor's yard.

"Shut up! You're a jerk!" I yelled back in an effort to sound tough but feeling embarrassed by the attention. The kid didn't have the courage to speak up again, so I concluded that my intimidating comeback was effective. However, it was also possible that he didn't continue his bullying because my parents chose to split up and my dad left our home soon after the incident.

To my knowledge, we were the first family on our street to have a broken home. The most pressing thing to my brother, sister, and me after we learned that Dad was leaving was who would get the bedroom he was using for his office. Maybe we focused on his belongings because we didn't understand the significance of what was happening, but I think it was more likely due to the fact that we didn't see much of Dad growing up. He wasn't the type of dad that took his kids fishing or to the movies. When trying to explain his absence years later, he said to me, "I do better with adults than babies." Once he left the house, it didn't feel too different than when he'd technically been living there. My top goal at the time was to make it clear to my brother and sister that as the oldest child, I called dibs on the bedroom/office.

Our economic status changed when my parents separated. When they were together, we were considered a middle-class family. When they divorced, our finances fell sharply. Mom struggled as a single parent. She got a job as a secretary and barely made ends meet with her minimum wage salary and the little Dad gave her for child support. She applied for food stamps and got my siblings and me on the free lunch program at school. For some reason, she refused to seek additional financial help through welfare, but I overheard her on several occasions crying on the phone to my dad about money. Through tears she would implore, "I just need a little money to buy the kids school clothes. I can't do this on my own. Can't you help out a little more? Won't you just send me an extra twenty-five dollars for the kids?"

Despite the difficulties, she continued to own our home and I never actually felt poor. Perhaps I was lucky that this was in the 1970s. At this time, kids from the middle class didn't have cell phones, cars, or lavish summer trips to Europe—at least, not the kids in my neighborhood. I really didn't understand the full hardship on my mom during this time.

As a young adult, I never gave much thought to how my childhood affected me, but as I reflect now, I realize that my childhood experiences made me desire three things: praise, a professional job, and a way to get out of Dodge. I started to meet these needs by going to college.

I was a good student as a kid. Early on I figured out that I got praise, particularly from my dad, for academic achievements. The only thing Dad ever asked me about in my personal life was school, and as a young adult, school was the only topic I ever called him about. Years later, when my family was visiting him at his lake house in New Hampshire, he told me about the high expectations he once had for me academically.

"I thought you were going to win a Nobel Prize," Dad said as he flipped the marinated chicken he was grilling for dinner. I was flattered by his belief that I could reach such heights but also a little skeptical. Was he joking?

He said, "My hopes were crushed the night you called and said you had failed a course." I had exaggerated. I got a C.

"Well, Dad," I said jokingly, "sorry to have disappointed you!" I knew that despite my inability to garner the attention of the Nobel Prize judges, I had succeeded in my academic career.

I selected a college I perceived as being focused on intellectual women, women who wanted careers. At the time, I thought the boys at my high school were not serious students, and I wanted nothing to do with their foolishness. I was intrigued by the brochures I received from a women's college a few states away that included pictures of women peering into microscopes. The college was a perfect fit for me. The small liberal arts college was several states south of Massachusetts and thus far enough away, and it focused on educating women. The college also had relationships with a prestigious coed university in the neighboring town and with a military academy down the road.

I used money saved from my after-school job, scholarships, and school loans to enroll at Goucher College in Towson, Maryland in the fall of 1978. I entered as a biology major and listed my career goal in the freshman register as "to be a physician." Not long after arriving on campus, I faced the reality that not all boys were stupid and silly.

Like many, my world view was broadened through my college experience. My sophomore year I was able to take a winter break course, Tropical Marine Biology, with about ten classmates in St. Croix, Virgin Islands. Besides scuba diving every day in the bright blue tropical waters, the course required skills in drinking Cruzan Rum and in dancing to calypso and reggae music. I learned that my dancing abilities improved with the more rum I drank. The following two years, I used the extended winter breaks to travel solo to Israel and then to Pakistan and India. I caught a bit of the travel bug while in college.

This wanderlust made me start to question my career goals. By my third year in college, when premed students typically take the medical school entrance exam, I started to struggle. I decided to talk with my organic chemistry teacher who had me as a student the previous year. He always made time for me, and while he wasn't officially my academic advisor, I saw him as a trusted mentor. Sitting in his office one afternoon, I found myself embarrassed by my lack of academic progress that semester. I avoided his eyes and rapidly blinked to stop my own eyes from tearing. "I don't know what's wrong with me. I haven't taken the med school exam and I just am floundering," I confessed.

In his warm, grandfatherly way, he responded, "Donna, have you thought about a career in public health? This might be a place to combine your interests in travel and in health."

This conversation changed my life.

After graduating college, I wasn't quite sure what to do next. I had no idea what public health was so it took me a while to internalize my professor's earlier insight. While considering my next step, I went back to Pakistan. During this time, I researched public health and decided to apply to graduate school. I reached out to my organic chemistry teacher to ask if he would write some letters of recommendation. He agreed and mailed me a note after he completed this task.

"Dear Donna, I've submitted the letters of recommendation for you. I have no doubt that you will get accepted into graduate school, and based on my notes, you might also hear from the Nobel Prize Committee. Best of luck."

My dad would be proud to know that receiving a call from the Nobel Prize Committee was still a possibility, yet I'm still waiting. I did, however, hear back from the graduate schools to which I applied. I got accepted.

In the fall of 1983, I enrolled in the Master of Public Health program at the University of North Carolina at Chapel Hill, studying public health nutrition. Actually, my interest was in malnutrition. Before classes started, I explored the campus. I walked over to the medical school student store, which at the time was not far from the School of Public Health. At this visit, I bought my first UNC sweatshirt and a book that captured my interest. The book was *Diarrhea and Malnutrition: Interactions, Mechanisms, and Interventions* (Chen and Scrimshaw, 1983). It is not likely to make it to any book club reading lists.

During my studies, I came to learn that nutrition was an awkward fit for me particularly since I tended to eat more than my share of fast food. However, the process of helping communities promote wellness and respond to health challenges fascinated me. My interest in global health subsided as I became involved in local campaigns to increase breast cancer awareness, to decrease tobacco use, and to prevent the spread of HIV and other infectious diseases. While working at my county public health department after graduation, I also became interested in crisis communication. Our department was involved in several high-profile crises and as the newbie to the team, I was volunteered by my colleagues to be the departmental media spokesperson. I found that I was energized by the excitement generated by crises. I later took this interest into my doctoral program in Public Health Leadership and did my doctoral research on crisis preparedness.

My husband and I met in our shared residence hall while we were in graduate school. He paid for his schooling by working as an assistant residence director, and as such had one of the two full apartments in the building. My roommate worked for him a couple times per week as the receptionist at the front desk in the lobby. When I visited her on the evenings that she worked, I saw my soon-to-be husband who was also in the office. Years later, my husband told me that one day when I walked past, he said to a friend that I was the woman he was going to marry. Despite this declaration, I was the one who made the first move toward dating.

One day, he walked into the resident hall with a bag of groceries. I happened to see him enter and decided to ask, "What's in the bag?" He told me he was making dinner for his boss, the residence director. I followed with another question: "When are you going to make me dinner?" After I put him on the spot, he said, "Don't say things that you don't mean." I flirted back, confirming that I wanted him to cook me dinner.

He made me a delicious chicken dinner that Friday night and we dated for eight years before we got married with our friends, colleagues, and family around us. We were in our late thirties when we became parents to two sons.

The next decade was filled with work, children, activities with friends and family, and finishing my dissertation. Each December, I summarized our family's achievements and challenges in an annual family news note, which served both as a family journal and as our holiday card for friends. In 1999, our note included the birth of our second son, the start of Montessori school for our older toddler son, the purchase of a new house, an award for most outstanding research paper for my husband, continued work for me in leadership development, and the passing of our pet, Miss Kitty.

Our 2003 note was shared in numbers: two 5K running races for me, seventy wet bed sheets changed, forty hours of guitar practiced by my husband, ten canopic jars and other ancient Egyptian artifacts made at summer camp, and twelve and a half years of marriage. Life was full, but after the year when our achievements included buying a silver van to fit the kids, dog, and friends, replaced the roof on our house, and declared the Iguanodon as the favorite house dinosaur, I started to think I needed to spice things up.

For the year leading up to my fiftieth birthday, 2009, I decided to engage in a personal challenge to experience fifty adventures by my milestone birthday. During this year, I went to Sudan, went skydiving, and ran a half marathon in North Carolina's Outer Banks. On the day of my actual fiftieth birthday, I found myself on a work trip in Tucson, Arizona and the friend I was staying with helped me reach adventure number twenty-five. She took me to a local tattoo parlor where I proceeded to have the Chinese word for crisis—which is often translated into two words: *danger* and *opportunity*—tattooed on my hip. Since I don't know the language, I assume that's what it says.

I learned that everyone has a different definition of the word adventure. Some want a rush of adrenaline while others want learning. In my quest, I wanted to include activities that were novel, fun, and made me feel fully alive. I didn't complete my goal of fifty adventures in the timeframe, but I knew I wanted the adventures to continue.

The question I faced after my fiftieth birthday was: Should I include "deal with progressive diseases" to my list of adventures?

CHAPTER 6.

The Monster: Anxiety

My heart stopped for a minute one day as I was talking with Eugene and he announced, "I can't help you."

We had been meeting for just a few months. On this particular day, I sat in my usual seat and started to drone on about how overwhelmed I felt by the items on my to-do list. I ran my own consulting business which allowed me to work with a variety of groups and organizations. The projects were always related to leadership development and I often juggled several clients at a time.

I typically enjoyed the work and the people I partnered with on each project. What I didn't enjoy was navigating the details and logistics of each project, particularly the administrative details. The various systems and processes like how to get paid, how to get reimbursed, and how to book travel were different for each client and not as intuitive as they each assumed. I'm the type of person who likes to jump into playing a new board game without reading the instructions first. Therefore, I never wanted to take the time to read the instructions for these systems. Instead, I just clicked randomly on links with the hope that I would somehow figure everything out.

In my ramble to Eugene that particular morning, I complained, "In order to get paid for the work that I did, I have to learn the company's payment system." Without stopping for a breath, I continued, "It is overwhelming me and I—"

He cut me off mid-sentence, as he often did. "Don't use the word *it*," he said. "*You* are overwhelming yourself."

"Well, it's just that if I want to get paid for the work I did, I need to learn a new system." I continued with my complaint as if more information might convince Eugene that "it" was overwhelming me.

I'm sure this conversation topic was about as interesting as watching paint dry on the wall, but the topic never mattered to Eugene no matter how drama rich. Filling out timesheets, parenting my kids, or arguing with my mother were just events. He was looking for themes in how I responded to these situations and whether or not I accepted how I responded to them.

"If you don't care if you get paid, just don't learn the system," he responded, using a reverse psychology technique he once told me he used with teenagers. Apparently, it worked on me as well. Did I want to invest in learning a new system so I could get paid? Of course I did.

I stared at Eugene as I processed our conversation. I saw him shift to lean forward in his chair. He rested his hands on his knees. That's when he said he couldn't help me. Actually, his exact words were, "I can't help you stop worrying."

Wait. Isn't that why I was here? Was my own therapist telling me I was hopeless? Was he suggesting that I find another therapist? If Eugene couldn't help me, who could? His words stung.

I did not want to live the rest of my life, however long it was going to be, having trouble concentrating, feeling like doom was around every corner, or envisioning myself hanging by my fingernails on the edge of a cliff. I sought therapy to stop worrying, to stop panicking, and to stop being overwhelmed. Could I be helped?

My recent medical diagnoses contributed to the dread I felt, but I also had a family history of worry and anxiety. Apparently, the apple hadn't fallen far from the tree.

My mom was a worrier. We jokingly called her Debbie Downer, given her propensity to connect every story to a catastrophe or worry. When I was a child, I recall her expressing concerns about any person who dared knock on our door to sell us a vacuum cleaner, encyclopedia set, or cleaning product. "They might rob us," she would say. With metal tray tables serving as our living room furniture, I was never quite sure what they would want to steal. Her warnings continued as I grew. One evening, I called her after I returned home from a work trip.

"Mom, I just got back from New York City."

"Oh, New York," she said in a tone that suggested a lecture was to follow. "Have you heard about the explosion of bedbugs in the hotels up there?" I mentally racked my brain to find a way to divert the conversation to a new topic. Unfortunately, I wasn't fast enough with a response. She continued, "You need to check your suitcase and clothes. You may have carried some of those bed bugs home."

"Thanks, Mom, for the insight," I sarcastically mumbled back.

Despite being raised by Debbie Downer, I don't recall being consumed with worry as a child. My childhood was spent running through the woods and zooming around on our plastic low-riding, Big Wheel tricycles through the pretend streets we made in the backyard by raking the fallen leaves. When I was a bit older and studying nutrition, I wondered if I had every nutritional deficiency that we learned about in class, but at the time, I believed that all medical and health students did this. I didn't see it as a sign that I was a worrier.

As a young adult, I even did things that made some people say I wasn't worried enough. Once, I drove roundtrip to Wisconsin, thirty hours total, on bald tires for a summer internship for my master's degree program. On a number of occasions, I also traveled alone to foreign countries. On one of my trips to Asia, during a layover in New York City, I disembarked long enough to have Tanzanian coffee at the home of the male passenger who sat next to me on the plane. Unfortunately, I told my mother about my side excursion. What was I thinking, both in doing it and by telling her? For the next forty years of business trips, she reminded me to not get off the plane and go off with strangers. "They could kill you," she repeatedly warned.

Signs that I was a worrier emerged more fully after I had children. Since I believed it was common for many moms to develop some anxiety, I didn't worry about my worrying. I also reasoned I was more on guard than others because both of my children had health issues early in life.

The types of things I worried about weren't just limited to my children, but again, I thought they were similar to things that concerned others. I worried about test taking and public speaking. I worried about getting scammed at the train station in Paris and about being exposed as an incompetent fraud at work. I worried that my kids might hang out with drug dealers, that they would drive dangerously along a mountain road during a rainstorm, and that they would bring home bedbugs from a trip.

Apparently, some people thought I worried a lot, including my oldest son. When he was a toddler, he expressed his feelings through a game of "What does the animal say?"

My husband asked him, "What does the doggie say?"
"Ruff, ruff."
"What does the cow say?"
"Moo, moo."
"What does the mommy say?"
"I'm so worried. I'm so worried."

Even though I insisted the joke was not funny, my husband laughed heartily then and every time he told it to others afterward.

The first time I realized I was changing my behaviors because of things that made me "nervous" was when I was being treated for Graves' disease, about four years prior to my scleroderma and lung disease diagnoses. Anxiousness and irritability can be problems related to thyroid issues, but even after my treatment ended and I was given a daily dose of replacement hormones, I could see I was starting to avoid situations that were becoming sources of fear, like driving.

Driving through tunnels, driving next to trucks or near the concrete blocks used to line highways under construction, being a passenger rather than the driver in a car, playing with the radio while driving, driving in the rain . . . need I go on? Gloom and doom and images worthy of any horror movie popped into my head. Visions of cars hanging precipitously over the edge of cliffs and bodies too bloodied to be identified played frequently on my internal screen. When this happened, my heart would start beating in my throat and I would frantically try to deflect the horrendous thoughts like a combatant in a Harry Potter fight scene. Needless to say, I found myself opting for the back seat on car trips when someone else was driving and planning my own trips to avoid travel routes that included tunnels, road construction, or bridges.

After I was diagnosed in 2015, my worry escalated as if it were on steroids. Unwanted, intrusive thoughts invaded my brain. These thoughts led to another concerning behavior.

Curled up one afternoon in my favorite spot on the sofa, I answered a phone call from my sister. At some point during our discussion, I disclosed that I was accumulating medicines, many of which I never even took after picking them up at the pharmacy. I didn't really like taking medicine. I didn't even want to take the necessary handful of pills that were considered the best therapeutic option for my conditions. However, I did like having the medicines. It comforted me to know that if my back went out again, I was ready. If I needed a stronger acid reflux medicine, I was ready. If I needed an antibiotic to counter my reduced immunity caused by my immunosuppressant drug, I was ready. My sister interrupted my description of the newest item being considered for my growing home pharmacy, nitroglycerin paste for my Raynaud's symptoms. Referring to my hoarding behavior, she interjected, "This is anxiety."

Immediately, I recognized that she was right. Initially, I felt amazed by the insight. Then, feelings of shame and disappointment swept over me. A familiar thought jumped into my head. *What's wrong with you?*

"Anxiety is energy with no place to go," Eugene said to me not long after my conversation with my sister. This made sense. Anxiety was trapped inside my body and it felt dangerous. I needed help letting it go. So I was taken aback when he had said that morning in his office that he could not help me stop worrying. Thankfully, I learned that he wasn't saying I was hopeless.

"My job now," he explained, "is to help you accept who you are."

PART II

Accepting the Now: Work Trip

"You look great! You've lost a lot of weight. Was it on purpose?"

The compliment came from a colleague who caught me in line at the hotel coffee shop. We were in Houston for a work-related project and I was meeting her and our other teammate in the lobby to carpool to the client's office. I wanted to grab a cup of caffeine to jump start the long day ahead of me.

With the exception of one or two people who were both coworkers and personal friends, nobody at work knew about my ailments. My health affected my time (lots of doctor appointments and periods of sickness), my energy, and some of my head space, but, fortunately, I could still work on small projects without having to disclose my personal challenges. The fact that I did most of my work from home helped. My home office provided me with a safe space to manage my own time and needs. I didn't want to lose work opportunities, so I kept struggles related to my health to myself.

As I stood in the middle of the coffee shop, I shifted my weight from one leg to the other. My first reaction was to not say anything or just say thank you for the compliment. Then I thought, *Go ahead. She cares about you. Tell her the truth.* I felt a level of discomfort, but I chose to be honest with her.

"Well, not on purpose." I opened the door to my secret. "I got diagnosed with an autoimmune disease and I was put on a new medicine. It's messing with my taste and eating habits."

I gave myself an imaginary kick. Did I really need to say all of that? Fortunately, I stopped before adding additional details about the side effects of my medicines and my health problems. We were standing in line at the hotel coffee shop, which was probably not the right place to mention gastrointestinal problems.

She stood motionless, not knowing how to respond at first. Then she said something like, "I'm sorry to hear this." I was in my head as she spoke, trying to find words that would convince both of us that I was still able to do the work we had scheduled for the day. "I'm fine," I assured her as I pointed to our other colleague who had just walked into the hotel lobby in search of us.

My "issues" were best managed by not eating much, so other than my morning coffee, I limited my food intake during the workday. At lunch time, I pushed my salad around on my plate and only sipped a couple spoonfuls from my bowl of soup. By the end of our long day of work, I was hungry. We decided to go out to eat and one of my colleagues, knowledgeable about the area, selected a local restaurant. Back at the hotel, we freshened up and agreed to meet again in the lobby for our dinner outing in ten minutes.

As we navigated a multi-lane highway to get to the chosen restaurant, a wave of nausea rose in my throat. Beads of sweat broke out on my forehead and I had a sudden urge to vomit. Unfortunately, this feeling was familiar. I knew I had approximately ten seconds before I made a mess in the rental car. I vomited two to three times per week, although it rarely occurred this early in the evening. It most often happened about an hour after taking the second dose of my medicine, anywhere between 9:00 p.m. and 11:00 p.m.

Only my husband knew the true extent of my GI struggles. Nausea and vomiting are secrets that many sick people keep to themselves unless they are too obvious to hide. I had vomited the previous night in my hotel room, so I was shocked by my need to do it again, particularly since I hadn't yet taken my nighttime medicines. This time, I had no way to hide the sick part of me.

Without time for an explanation, I opened my purse and pulled out some wadded plastic grocery bags. I placed them up to my mouth and I vomited. The noise of me retching in the back seat alerted my colleagues that something was wrong. In response, my colleague who was driving exited the mega-highway and navigated us to a side street where we could park. By the time we stopped the car, I felt better. I wiped my mouth with a wet wipe, which I also had stored in my purse, tied up my double-bagged vomit and tried to assure my colleagues that I was good to go.

"I'm so sorry," I said, horrified by what I had just done.

"Are you okay? Should we go back to the hotel?" my workmates asked with genuine concern.

"No, no," I said, waving my hand to indicate we should continue. "I'm good. Let's go."

Meanwhile, I wondered if the back seat could lift so I could crawl under the car and disappear.

We got back on the highway and arrived at a busy family-style restaurant. I threw my package away in a trash can at the entry way to the restaurant and excused myself to freshen up. As I entered the restroom, a mother was changing the diaper of a wriggling toddler on a changing table and a woman was washing her hands at one of the sinks. I combed my hair, brushed my teeth, and wiped my face with a wet towel. Nothing remained of my illness.

Fortunately, I had all I needed to pull myself together. Packing "just-in-case" items had become one of my routines. Toothbrush and tooth paste, trash bags, extra socks and underwear, breath mints, tums, pills for any possible ailment, and one or two little hottie hand warmers were all stored in different compartments in my purse.

I returned to the table and ate my food, pretending like it was just another business trip dinner. My colleagues did the same, which I am forever grateful for. When I returned to the safety of my own hotel room, I wondered what impact my openness that morning had on how we handled the unexpected event that evening. In some small way, I felt relief.

A few months later, my colleagues hired me for another team project and Facebook started sending me ads for emesis bags.

CHAPTER 7.

How Are You?

I don't know how I am.

How are you? or *How are you doing?* are common superficial greetings used in the US upon meeting or seeing a friend, colleague, or acquaintance. The person asking often doesn't care to hear the real answer and the person being asked often doesn't want to give a real answer. These questions are typically used to acknowledge a person's presence. They're not really asked in service of soliciting a real answer about someone's quality of life.

The greeting *How are you?* often becomes *How are you feeling?* once the person asking the question is aware that the person they are asking is ill, is going through a challenge, or has just experienced some other life-altering event. For someone who is struggling the question may feel just as hollow despite the word change, particularly if asked at the produce counter in the grocery store or in the conference room before a meeting starts. No one wants to cry or tell you about their suffering over the eggplant in the store or while the agenda is being passed around at the meeting.

After my diagnoses, I suddenly found myself having trouble answering these questions. I didn't know what people were truly asking me. Were they asking me about my illness, my physical issues, my emotional status, or were they asking me about my kids, my work, or my husband? Were they asking about how I was at that moment or in general? Did they really want to know how I was or were they just using the question as a greeting?

Before my life turned upside down or before I turned my life upside down, I would answer these questions with "I'm fine" or "We're fine. How are you?" I didn't think anything of the question nor of my answer. I was answering in general, which meant that after a quick mental scan of the last two to three months, we, my family, were fine. No major events had taken place.

Now, every minute felt different. My mood and physical self-assessment went up and down depending on what was happening at that moment. I felt like I was on a roller coaster. For example, one minute I could have a little problem swallowing a cracker. The slightly chewed cracker might sit a second or two longer than usual in the back of my throat. This perceived delay in swallowing would trigger me to create intrusive thoughts like, *This is a sign that your GI tract is no longer working. The scleroderma has advanced. You'll need to switch to baby food soon.* I was not fine in that moment.

A minute later, I might become distracted and suddenly forget my gagging and unsettling thoughts. At that point, if you asked, "How are you?" I would "feel fine" and I would say so. But for a second, I would also wonder if I should tell you that I might need to move to a soft food diet soon. Trying to figure out what I should or wanted to tell people about my status was exhausting.

Eugene advised me to speak my mind and not worry about how much or how little I was saying. If I provided specifics to people, then I must have needed to tell someone details at that precise time. He advised me to mimic the well-known radio host Paul Harvey, whose signature tagline was, "And now you know the rest of the story" (Harvey 2022), if I did wish to talk about what I was going through. Eugene assigned me some introductory sentences to rehearse as homework.

"'Let me tell you where I am right now,' or 'Let me tell you what's happening to me right now.'"

Sometimes, I kicked myself for oversharing even if I did need to talk. Once on a work trip to Oakland, California, after an exhausting day-and-a-half meeting, a colleague and I decided to use the remainder of our trip to drive to Napa Valley to see some vineyards and have dinner. We put our work bags stuffed with materials from our meeting into the trunk of her rental car, hopped into the front seats, and began the one-hour drive. I hadn't seen her in years, so when she asked how I had been, I shared my health journey. I immediately felt that I had overshared. My internal voice popped into my head and started complaining, *Why would you put such a wet blanket over such a nice afternoon? She doesn't want to know all of the details of your gut health and breathing issues.* I was trying to talk and shut myself up at the same time.

My colleague, a physician and generally nice person, listened to me and expressed sadness that I had been struggling. After a while, I stopped talking about my illnesses and experiences with the medical system, but I felt as if I could have gone on for hours. Once I started sharing, I didn't know where to stop. Asking me *How are you?* was like opening Pandora's box. Eventually, my friend and I made it to Napa and had a lovely dinner. Still, I kicked myself for bringing up such a heavy subject on such a fun evening.

Another exchange that sticks with me involves a text message my brother sent me one day. After learning the seriousness of my condition, he started to send me texts asking, "How are you feeling?" While I appreciated that he was thinking of me, I always wondered when he sent me a text, *What is the appropriate response to this question in this shallow medium?* On this occasion, he asked me how I was feeling and gave me a personal update, which I felt also required a response. I probably should have just said that I was fine and focused on his announcement.

"Hey Don, just checking in to see how are you feeling? BTW, did you hear the news? Nicole and I are getting married."

I texted back, "Congratulations! I saw your FB post. I'm tired from my recent lung test and the stomach issues from meds, but these issues are normal for me. Big visit to Duke Hospital on Wed, but again, it's all normal. Thx for asking."

My discomfort with this exchange was in the mixing of topics, particularly topics that were at different ends of the news spectrum, as anyone except Eugene might classify them. My brother seemed fine with my response, but I thought he didn't really care how I was doing. I also felt awkward by congratulating him on his engagement while also announcing that I had diarrhea. He deserved more than that.

Some people who are going through a difficult time, like those in cancer treatment, say to the loved ones who thoughtfully keep in touch, "Please stop asking me how I am or how I'm feeling." Naturally, the loved ones ask with the best of intentions, but they are unaware of how challenging it can be for the person going through a difficult time to respond, especially if they're asked again and again.

Loved ones or friends may also request updates not often enough or not at all. As I reflect on my own behaviors, I recognize that some of my past responses to other people's challenges, such as hovering or ghosting the person, have been rooted in either my inability to witness loved ones struggle or my lack of understanding of how to help.

Once, I avoided a family I'd grown to care for after tutoring their son in science for the better part of a year. The father was rapidly declining in health. After my tutoring responsibilities were over, I never contacted the family again. I didn't know what to say, and to this day I feel tremendous guilt and shame over my response or lack thereof.

With maturity, I came to understand that regularly reaching out to loved ones going through a tough time is important to the loved one and to the friend who is reaching out, but *How are you?* is not always the right question. Now, if a friend is struggling, I send an occasional text or voice message that says, "I'm thinking about you!" or "What you are going through is difficult," or "If you need something, let me know. I can fold laundry, do errands, pick up the kids, drive over with a shot of whiskey, do research on doctors and treatments, or just call every once in a while." Personally, I have appreciated receiving these kinds of messages.

I also appreciate the friends who continued to check on me for years, well beyond the initial crisis phase of learning about my diagnoses. Several friends spontaneously send texts and others send me socks and gloves in the mail. I also have friends that call every few months out of the blue to ask, "How are you right now?" One such friend called me one afternoon in March 2018, two and half years after my diagnoses. Her call changed the course of my day.

March had been particularly exhausting and stressful for me. I had scheduled more medical tests and procedures than usual because I had become fearful that my health was declining. To check my status, my doctors ordered several tests including a CT scan of my lungs, multiple blood tests, an echocardiogram, a colonoscopy with biopsies (as a result of my fears about my GI system), and a bronchoscopy. The first several tests were familiar to me, but the bronchoscopy was new. Dr. Lung ordered it to rule out a lung infection.

The bronchoscopy required that I lie on a hospital bed in a sterile surgery room, have anesthetic gel squirted up my nose, and have a tube glided through my nose into my lung. I was given an intravenous sedative so I don't remember most of the procedure, but I was fully awake throughout the process of numbing my nose and throat. In her effort to calm me, the medical technician mentioned as she shoved a syringe up one nostril, "Some people feel as if they can't breathe once their passages are numbed, but I assure you that you can." As she said this, I began to gasp. A familiar feeling of panic started to rise in my chest. I think I would still have PTSD from this test if I hadn't had to get back on the horse for a similar procedure a year later that ended up being less stressful.

The anticipation of medical tests and receiving results from those tests, as well as the physical burden of going to the clinic or hospital to *do* the tests, was taxing. At the end of the month after all of the tests and procedures, I found myself battling my thoughts.

Despite knowing that calling a friend was a helpful strategy for getting past times of emotional struggle, I did not call anyone. I yelled at myself instead for a few days. *You should be able to handle the symptoms and tests that go a long with your progressive disease, as well as the intrusive thoughts that you generate. All of this is not new! For Christ sake, get a grip!*

Fortunately, after my second or third day of self-flagellation, the phone rang. A friend was calling me.

Not knowing anything about my month of testing, she said, "I've been thinking about you. How are you right now?"

"I've been struggling," I said.

"Why didn't you reach out for support?" she inquired, sounding disturbed by my answer. "So many of us love you and want to help."

I had convinced myself that my mental health "pity parties" were not a good enough reason to reach out to friends week after week, month after month, and year after year. My situation was no longer new. How long was it reasonable to reach out to others because I couldn't handle things?

"I was embarrassed that I couldn't work through the negative thoughts on my own after so much therapy. I didn't want to continue to be a burden on my friends," I confessed.

"You have hardly called on any of us!" she admonished. "Speaking for myself, I don't feel burdened. And even still, we're your friends. Lean on us as much as you need to, for as long as you need to." I could feel myself being lifted as she spoke.

In addition to my friends, Eugene was also an invaluable support to me that week. He had been pressing me to become more aware of myself as I experienced the moment in front of me, the "now." When I walked into his office for my appointment around that time, he asked me how I was. When he asked, I knew he was asking me how I was, in *my body*, at that moment.

"I feel like static electricity is running through me. I can't control it. I want it to stop."

"You are doing this to yourself," Eugene said emphatically.

"No," I countered. "It's automatic."

"Who's doing it to you? Is the chair that you're sitting in causing the electricity?" he pushed back, moving his arms around to appear more animated. "Accept that this is what your body does, and then relax."

Now, when I am heading for a panic attack, I blame it on the chair I'm sitting in and not my mind. Then I purposely relax and say out loud, "Donna, it is what it is. You become electric when you stress yourself and if you want to dim the charge, call a friend. They will ask you how you're doing and you can say anything you feel that you need to say. They are your friend and they will know that listening is the gift you need."

CHAPTER 8.

Am I in the Fight?

———

The question hung over me persistently: *Should I seek another opinion?*

Scleroderma Centers of Excellence existed in various medical centers around the country, I'd learned. Duke Health, which was about an hour's drive from my home, had one of these specialized clinics.

Duke Health, located in Durham, North Carolina, is like any other major medical system—a city of buildings with tunnels above and below ground that patients must navigate to find the location of their appointment. The Scleroderma Clinic was located at the end of the hallway with the purple elevators in Duke South. Finding the right clinic was like walking through the shrub maze in the movie *The Shining* (1980). Similar to the shrub-lined pathways in the movie, all the hallways and clinics looked the same. Seeing a patient and their caregiver standing in the middle of a hallway trying to figure out where they were and where they needed to go was not uncommon. As I walked these halls for my first few appointments, I had no clue if I was getting closer or further away from where I needed to be.

A phone app with a hospital version of the backyard game Hot and Cold would be helpful for navigating this huge hospital city, particularly on your first visits. As you walked, the app could be programmed to say, "You're getting warmer" or "You're getting colder. Re-calc-u-lating." At least there would be some indication that you were or were not in the right building and moving in the right direction.

It took me at least four months to get an appointment with one of the highly recommended physicians in the Scleroderma Clinic, Dr. Scleroderma. I remember thinking, "I could be dead by the time I get to see this specialist." Thankfully, I didn't die and I learned that he was worth the wait.

On my first visit, Dr. Scleroderma, who I will also call Dr. SSc, provided my husband and me a master class on scleroderma, information on a local support group, and an invitation to explore enrollment in an upcoming clinical trial for a possible new drug for scleroderma patients, OFEV. The meeting was informative, but I felt overwhelmed. At the end of the visit, I asked the doctor, "What are the three main messages you want me to leave with?" Without hesitation, he answered:

- "It will be important to closely monitor your heart and lungs; you will need an echocardiogram, for instance, once a year.
- You should frequently and routinely monitor your blood pressure as an indication of kidney health.
- Scleroderma doesn't define you."

Initially, I wanted to see Dr. SSc because he was a scleroderma expert. Scleroderma is a rare disease; even physicians who have heard of it haven't treated a patient and don't really know much about it. As I got to know Dr. SSc, I recognized that he checked all of the boxes in the fictitious job description I created for my doctors. He was knowledgeable about the science, he attended the local volunteer-led scleroderma support group to learn how people "live" with this illness, he communicated well, he led research studies to push for better treatments, he was punctual, he was interested in me beyond my health, and he was young.

After interacting with so many doctors, I also started to identify characteristics and behaviors I did not want. Dr. Thyroid had demonstrated a lack of punctuality and questionable medical competence. I certainly didn't want those characteristics. A local gastroenterologist who I saw immediately after being diagnosed said, "I don't know much about scleroderma except that the GI tracks of these patients become lead pipes that don't move." This statement is true, but it was presented in a way that I was unable to take in at the time. I didn't want someone on my team who wasn't aware of how scared people process information.

A third physician said he could include me as a patient in his practice, but I should be aware that his wife was pushing him to make more time for travel and retirement. I also graded him lower after an insensitive remark about my recent weight gain, saying it made me look like I had been put on steroids.

All of these doctors were nice enough, but I needed doctors who were competent and compassionate, doctors who didn't have one foot out the door. Also, if you call me fat, you're fired. Assuming that Dr. SSc didn't move, decide on a career change like becoming a chef or comedian, or have his own health event, I told myself that he would outlive me and would be with me for the whole journey.

About six months after my first appointment in the Scleroderma Clinic, Dr. SSc informed me that the OFEV study was ready to enroll patients. As the principle investigator for this study at Duke Health, he explained the research goals and expectations.

OFEV is a drug that has expanded the treatment options and average life expectancy for people who have progressive scarring in their lungs from an unknown cause known as idiopathic pulmonary fibrosis (IPF). A new worldwide clinical drug trial was scheduled to test the impact of this drug on people with interstitial lung disease with a known cause: scleroderma. The study was a one-year, double-blind randomized trial which meant that even the doctors didn't know if their patients were receiving the study medicine or the placebo pill. The hope was that OFEV would slow the progression of lung fibrosis in people with scleroderma as it was doing in people with IPF.

Dr. SSc made sure I understood every aspect of the study including the testing requirements, the schedule for taking the medicine each day, and the potential side effects of the medicine. He stressed the fact that participants could withdraw from the study at any time and could also be withdrawn for reasons, such as inability to tolerate the medicine or testing schedule. If I were to be enrolled in the study, I needed to have several medical tests to confirm my eligibility and then would need to sign a lengthy consent form. I began to gain an appreciation for all the people who have served as guinea pigs for pharmaceutical science.

After my appointment, my husband and I talked about the potential pros and cons of being in a clinical drug trial:

Pros

- The drug may halt or improve my lung disease
- The drug may slow the progression of my lung disease
- I would be contributing to science
- Other scleroderma patients with lung disease may be helped by knowledge gained from this study
- I will see a scleroderma specialist, Dr. SSc, on a regular basis
- Medical tests related to the study and the drug or placebo would be free during the study
- If given the placebo drug, I would be eligible to get OFEV after the first phase of the study prior to its availability to the public

Cons

- The drug may cause harm to my liver or to other parts of my body
- The visits to Duke will be time consuming and exhausting
- I don't know if I will actually get the study drug
- The study might show the drug doesn't work; it might be a waste of time
- I might not tolerate the side effects of the drug and could get kicked out of the study
- The strict protocol for taking the drug and monitoring its effects may be too restrictive for my lifestyle
- I may not tolerate the frequent testing requirements
- The drug may interfere with other drugs that I am taking

My husband encouraged me to participate in the study. He said, "I think you should consider the treatment options the experts suggest."

He had always wanted me to fight these illnesses. I recall one afternoon a few months before listing the pros and cons of the OFEV study. We sat out on the back deck of our house and my husband said to me, "We're going to fight this." I surprised myself with my response.

"No. I'm not going to fight this," I said. We sat in silence, each in our own thoughts.

While I didn't expand on what I was thinking during our brief conversation, I'll clarify it now.

At the time, I was already exhausted. The thought of a fight with scleroderma made me more tired. Fighting or being in battle is a common metaphor used by people who have been diagnosed with an illness, like cancer. I thought if I used this framing, I would likely come out as the loser. I could just hear the eulogy: "It's so sad. She lost her battle with interstitial lung disease and scleroderma."

When I declared that I wasn't going to fight, I wasn't waving a white flag. I just didn't want to prolong my ending by trying one more toxic drug, being hooked up to one more life-saving machine, hanging one more crystal over my head, or undergoing one more surgery that might help. I didn't want to view my life as a battle to be won. I just wanted to accept what was happening, use the available treatments as I wanted, and focus on enjoying whatever time I have left on this planet.

That being said, the biologist and public health specialist in me connected with the possibility of contributing to science and the well-being of others. What could be more important than leaving the world a better place than when you arrived? With these thoughts in my head, I consented to participation in the study during my next visit with Dr. SSc.

CHAPTER 9.

Controlling the Uncontrollable

"Where is the diarrhea? Shouldn't I be experiencing runny stools and cramping? Why don't I have diarrhea?" These questions started to emerge in my head. Since diarrhea is the last frontier of polite conversation, I initially kept the questions to myself. But I knew they reflected a new concern. I did not have diarrhea and I thought I should.

Can you imagine wanting diarrhea? Why would anyone want that?

Let me explain. I knew diarrhea was a very common side effect of the medicine being tested in the clinical drug trial I had just joined. Each day after being enrolled in the study, I expected that it would come. When it didn't, I was devastated.

Three weeks after starting the medicine I was given, I told the doctor, "I think I am on the placebo pill." With no sign of diarrhea, I concluded I must be eating sugar pills twice a day.

My doctor patiently listened and then explained, "People respond in different ways to OFEV. Not having new symptoms does not mean you were placed in the control group for the study." At that moment, I believed my own thoughts over the medical information my doctor shared.

Unfortunately, by believing my thoughts I created a lot of distress for myself. I not only believed I was not receiving the medicine, but I also believed the medicine saved lives. I had no proof that either of my thoughts were true, yet I began using them to make conclusions as if I was doing an algebra problem. If a=b and b=c, then a=c. If I'm not getting the medicine and the medicine is lifesaving, then not getting the medicine means my disease will quickly progress to death.

As my doctor started to rise from the desk chair at the end of the appointment, he asked, "Do you have any more questions?" I had a knot in my throat and tears welled up in my eyes. I was scared, but I had to ask the question sitting at the bottom of my stomach.

"Are you *sure* that we are doing all we can?"

His tone of voice lowered slightly and his eyes looked directly into mine, making me feel heard and cared for.

"Yes," he answered. "We are."

Before I joined the study, I kept an Excel spreadsheet of my symptoms for each body part. In the chart, I recorded issues with my hair, memory, eyes, teeth/gums, muscles, and skin. I continued down my body to the soles of my feet, which are cold and bluish-purple in color as I sit at my desk right now. Before joining the clinical trial, I had written in this chart that my gastrointestinal symptoms included acid reflux and an occasional bout of loose stool, which I attributed to a recent trip overseas. With this record in hand, I knew the frequency of any of my current symptoms had not gotten worse over the first few weeks of taking the study medicine.

The study protocol also required that patients be diligent about recording any issues they were experiencing, like changes in bowel habits, headaches, heart rhythms, or eating habits. Due to this request, I started also keeping a log sheet of when and how often I had bowel movements, just like you would with a newborn infant. As a result, I gained expertise in using the Bristol Stool Chart—or "poop chart," as I like to refer to it—a visual representation of at least seven categories of human excrement.

By the fourth month in the study I started to notice some changes. I could no longer eat baked goods like muffins or cakes because they tasted strange, and I noticed the frequency of diarrhea had slightly increased. Reflux was also still an issue, but I also had started to occasionally vomit. Given these changes, I scheduled a consultation with a new gastroenterologist.

The gastroenterologist stated that it was not clear what was causing the issues I was now experiencing. It could be a side effect from one or more of my other prescriptions, the advancement of my scleroderma, or the fact that I was taking the actual research drug. He advised me to first submit a stool sample to rule out any potential infections. I believed the changes were due to the worsening of my disease. My gut was becoming a lead pipe just like my first GI doctor told me it would. I could see it in my mind's eye.

My ability to turn information or even the lack of information into a full-blown horror story with frightening dialogue, haunting images, and scary music was remarkable. The nagging voice in my head became louder as I tried to interpret the increasing presence of my annoying symptoms. *Here I am*, scleroderma said. *You can't get away from me.*

The word *progressive*—used to characterize my illness—fueled my fantasies and negative self-talk. Even when a new issue arose such as those related to normal aging, I interpreted it as disease progression. As a result, I started having terrifying ideas and visions—basically, nightmares. One such image started occurring after I had convinced myself that my GI system was beginning to fail. The thought was horrifying. In a black-and-white scene, I was in a line walking to a gas chamber. I felt myself searching for a way out of the line but continued to inch slowly forward, following those in front of me. I wore rags. The smell of gas was becoming stronger and stronger. Children hung on my legs. I cried.

This overwhelming picture, straight off of a movie screen, showed in my head repeatedly for months during this time. My disease was progressive and I had no way to get out of the march toward death.

Even though Dr. SSc did not know which study group I had been placed in, medicine or placebo, he had to treat me as if I was taking the study drug. This meant ensuring that my liver and body were tolerating the medicine. He also had to treat me as if I was *not* on the medicine. This meant we had to assume my new symptoms were related to my disease or my other medicines. Therefore, over the next couple of months after I started to be concerned about my gut, I was scheduled for a colonoscopy with biopsies, a liver ultrasound, a lactulose hydrogen breath test, and an upper endoscopy. I learned that my colon was fine, my liver was slightly fatty, I didn't have an excessive amount of bacteria in my bowel, and I had some chronic gastritis. No lead pipe was visible.

As the new symptoms increased in frequency, they became harder to manage. At one point, I began wondering, "At what point is diarrhea, vomiting, and testing worse than being dead?" I now know that the worrying is worse than death. All the rest I can handle. At the time, however, I began counting my annoyances and losses.

People with chronic illnesses experience a lot of loss. This can lead to a perpetual sense of grief. I believed that I had lost many of the things that gave me joy. I sulked for months, for instance, when I finally decided that I needed to stop drinking coffee because it led to more acid reflux. I listed some of my losses in my journal during a Meeting to Worry.

- Ability to plan my future and any new adventures
- Travel to places that were high altitude or cold
- Ability to see future grandchildren
- Caffeinated coffee and late-night eating
- Interest in work
- Ability to exercise or be active

Adding "loss of control over my bodily functions" to my list was a tough pill to swallow. It never occurred to me to challenge any of my assumptions about my losses. I just started asking the universe, "What's next? What's next?"

On my next visit to see Eugene, I said, "I just feel like I don't have any control."

"That's not a feeling. You're creating a thought," he said in hopes that I would recognize the difference in the two.

Then he said, "And you never had any control to begin with."

Accepting that I had little control became a key lesson in my wellness journey, but at this point, it seemed like a cruel joke. It terrified me. My internal dialogue demonstrated that I wasn't quite receptive to the idea.

One day as I was driving home from a Duke hospital appointment, my mind wandered. I considered the extent to which people lose control at the end of life. I had a strange dialogue with myself.

In the end, when I am bedridden, will I have any control whatsoever? I wondered. *Let's say that I am upset with my caretaker but can't speak or move. Will I have any way to voice my displeasure?*

My other self said, *You could decide to shit your pants so your caretaker has to clean you up. That would show them you still had some control over the situation.*

I laughed at my brilliance until it occurred to me that my caretaker might decide not to clean me up, and then what? Who was in control at that point?

This grossed me out and I decided it wasn't such a good fantasy after all. People who are sick think weird thoughts.

At the end of the first phase of the clinical drug trial, one and half years after I was enrolled, I learned you should be careful what you wish for. I wanted diarrhea and I got it. I also learned that my taste aversions, diarrhea, headaches, and vomiting were due to being on the trial drug, OFEV, and not due to my scleroderma. The study demonstrated that OFEV *is effective* at slowing the progression of interstitial lung disease in people with scleroderma, at least in the first year of taking it (Distler et al. 2019, 380).

The medicine is now available to all people with scleroderma and lung disease. I'm working to accept that my body functions differently now and I will have diarrhea as long as I continue to take this medicine. To this I say, "Please pass the Imodium."

CHAPTER 10.

I'm Pissed at You

———

One day as I headed to an appointment with Eugene, I realized I didn't want to talk. My mind was racing and I felt overly emotional. I envisioned that talking to him would be like cutting myself open and exposing my beating heart to the world.

As I trudged the eleven steps to his office, I took note of my breathing. Testing my ability to climb steps was a habit I started as soon as I was diagnosed with lung disease.

Eugene opened the door as if he heard me coming. We greeted each other at the top of the steps and I walked by him to enter his office. I sat in the familiar rocking chair, which was placed directly in front of his chair about four feet away.

"Today," I announced, "I have a black cloud over my head."

The clinical drug trial had started a few weeks prior and I had convinced myself I was placed in the placebo group. To me, this meant the growing presence of GI issues was not related to the study drug but was actually a sign that my health was declining. In the end, none of my assumptions were true, but at the time, the new concerns just added to the heaviness I felt.

Believing that speaking one more word would be like pulling the wrong block in a game of Jenga, I sat frozen, staring at the floor. *Just hold it together*, my internal voice demanded. If only I could wrap myself in duct tape.

Eugene and I sat in the silence, something he was very comfortable doing but which, typically, I was not. Suddenly, without warning, he broke into a rap song, complete with leg slapping and foot tapping.

"I'm not gonna take this shit no more," thumpa, thumpa, clap, thumpa, thumpa, clap. I'm not gonna take this shit no more." He repeated the line with the sound effects.

He encouraged me to add some lyrics and beat sounds. *This is ridiculous* was my first thought. But I trusted that there was a method to his madness, so I considered his request.

Many times, our conversations were unusual, at least in my eyes. Once, Eugene repeatedly commanded me to say "I'm getting sicker!" while increasing my volume each time until I was screaming it. To capture the moment, I wrote in big letters in my journal, "I'm getting sicker, I'm Getting Sicker, I'M GETTING SICKER." While I may have understood the purpose of the request at the time, by the time I wrote about it in my journal, I also wrote, "Why did Eugene have me do this?"

Even if I didn't know the purpose of his interruptions or our discussions in the moment, I felt confident that he had a reason for steering us in the direction that he did. I always left his office thinking, which of course was what I was trying to do less of—but the reflecting after our discussions often led to powerful insights. An example of this was the time when I finally understood why he kept steering me, mid-sentence, away from using certain words. I had to start recognizing what I was doing and believing. My word choice was important in doing this.

Screaming "I'm getting sicker" and avoiding words like *it*, *wish*, and *should* were easy requests. Singing was entirely different. My confidence in my musical abilities was low particularly when I compared my level of talent to Eugene's level of musical talent. He was a musician. He played multiple instruments including the drums and had once been a member of a band before hazards of the occupation, such as late nights in bars, provided reasons to take a new direction. I, on the other hand, was not a musician and viewed myself as having no musical rhythm. Heck, my heart couldn't even keep a consistent beat!

With less gusto than Eugene, I finally complied with the invitation to join him in creating a rap song. First, I copied him.

"I'm not gonna take this shit no more. I'm not gonna take this shit no more."

Then I added my own refrain. "This sucks! It really, really sucks." I might have even added in some leg slapping and foot tapping. Eugene snapped his fingers and bounced his head as if he were a backup singer. Despite his enthusiasm, I was under no illusion that I was Jay-Z or Snoop Dogg. More embarrassed than pleased with myself, I stopped my part of the duet after my feeble attempt.

"I don't have any rhythm," I confessed, in case it wasn't obvious.

"Of course you do!" he said emphatically. "Rhythms can change at any time. You are changing your rhythm as you make music."

My facial expression demonstrated my skepticism.

"That doesn't mean you don't have rhythm. You're just not taking ownership of your rhythm," he said.

I enjoyed that Eugene often caught me off guard with his direct and unique approach to conversations. In this instance, the sudden rap song snapped me into being more present. I felt able to become part of a conversation, as if he had shocked my heart back to life. Oddly, my response to this event was similar to the time I had to stop a food fight between my sons. The distraction seemed to cure my rumination over a bad presentation I had made at work earlier that day. Distraction, it appears, is a powerful strategy for redirecting my attention away from the negative thoughts that keep looping around in my head.

It wasn't immediately obvious why Eugene was singing at the time. Whatever he set out to do, he eventually managed to connect the exercise to one of my challenges. I wasn't taking responsibility for my rhythm and, more importantly, for the misery and despair I was creating.

"I feel like my head is filled with a tangled, messy ball of yarn. I can actually see it." I paused for a second, then continued, "It feels chaotic and dense."

"Be that ball of yarn," he said. "Tell me about you, as that ball of yarn."

"There are many strands of yarn, not just one strand," I said, pushing aside my inclination to dismiss his statements as *so therapist*. "The strands are various colors and they are tangled, knotted, lumpy, and messy. I don't know how to untangle the strands."

"What are the strands?" he inquired.

I started listing: declining health; my prognosis; Mom's health; Dad's death; family; kids wanting more independence; jealousy of others planning travel adventures; work and lack of clarity around future work; wasting the time I have left; being lazy.

"And how are you communicating with others about these issues and your feelings?" he asked, taking the conversation down another unexpected road. Was he tired of me listing my grievances or was he just throwing spaghetti at the wall to see what topic would help me cross a bridge?

"I'm not communicating anything, at least not in any depth," I responded although unsure I wanted to go in this direction. I sank a little lower in the rocking chair. "I feel that if I open up any discussion it will result in an explosion of epic proportions, exaggerating my response."

"What do you mean?" he pushed me to continue.

"I'm afraid that asking, 'Who left the butter out on the counter?' will actually come out as 'Fuck you for leaving food out all over the house!'"

Not the least bit concerned I might blow up over a stick of butter being left on the counter, he said, "So you're squashing your feelings to spare others from the explosion of feeling, but the stress that's coming from bottling up those feelings may be making your disease worse?"

"Yes." I suddenly envisioned scleroderma dumping cement in to the cells of my blood vessels as I let stress consume me.

"When you were talking about your ball of yarn, I felt myself tighten up. But as you were pulling each thread out to describe it, I felt myself loosen up," he said, adding, "Hm. I also recognized that I felt some anger."

"Anger?" I asked, curious to know what he meant.

"Yes. Anger, that you are doing this to yourself," he explained calmly, not actually showing his anger in his tone or in his facial expression.

This got my attention. I sat up in the chair a little higher. "You're pissed at me?" I asked.

"Yes, I guess as you say, I was a little pissed at you."

He smiled and I started to laugh. We had worked together long enough that I knew he was telling me what he truly felt, but I also knew he was pissed in the most kind and caring way. He was always brutally honest, which in turn made me more honest during our discussions. We continued to chat about some actions I could take to untangle the mass of yarn I had created until my sixty-minute session with him was over.

Despite the intense conversation that day, I would have to be reminded over and over again what I was doing to myself and how to stop. I started by accepting my "different" rhythm.

CHAPTER 11.

The Glass Is Half Full!

The dinner conversation was typical until it wasn't.

My girlfriends and I had gone out to eat. Eight of us had been meeting regularly for dinners and beach trips for the last fifteen years. Three members of our group didn't join us this evening due to work or home commitments. These were very busy women. I valued whatever time we had together and felt grateful that they had been so supportive during my health journey.

For the most part, we met through our children, who attended the same local school. One evening when our kids were toddlers, Jane invited us all to dinner. She and I had met after her two-year-old daughter and my two-year-old son formed a fast friendship in the sandbox behind the school. I also knew Laura. Laura and her husband both worked with my husband and we once shared a nanny when our oldest sons were babies. Jane's first dinner invitation introduced me to most of the other women. That first night we talked about balancing busy careers and motherhood.

On this particular night, we met at a small local restaurant that served Mediterranean food. The restaurant was more casual than our usual dining picks, but since we wanted to expand our exploration of Greensboro's dining scene, we decided to try it. Most of the restaurant's business was takeout, which was ordered at a counter in the front of the establishment. The dining room in the back serviced about six to eight small parties. The tables were standard pressed wood squares on top of cast iron table bases. The chairs were black metal with laddered backs, stackable but not suitable for long periods of sitting. We pushed three table squares together to accommodate our group on this night. I remember feeling that the lighting in the room was too bright for evening dining. It felt more like a college dining hall than a fine dining room. But it didn't matter; friend time was the point.

We each ordered our meals at the front counter. I ordered the vegetarian sampler (hummus, tabbouleh, spinach pie, falafel, olives, and spice-dusted pita slices), which reminded me of a visit I made to Israel while I was in college. One by one we went to the beverage station located on a counter at the entrance of the dining area. We filled our glasses and then sat at the tables we had claimed.

We fell quickly into conversation and ultimately moved into our typical routine of going around in a circle to check in with each person. Over the years, our updates and conversations focused on the challenges and rewards of raising kids. Occasionally, we also talked about upcoming trips or changes in spousal relationships. In 2017, we started talking about getting our teens into or through college and helping some of our elderly parents transition to the end of life. Plastic surgery came up a time or two, but we hadn't yet entered the phase where we were discussing the level of sexiness of adult diapers (this conversation was soon to come, but not on this night).

The summer had been busy for me. I had recently finished some work projects and had just been asked about being part of a team for a project in Madagascar, which my doctor encouraged me to do. My youngest had recently graduated from high school and was preparing to enter college, and the previous week I had signed up for ten ballroom dancing sessions at the local Fred Astaire Dancing Studio. Despite all of these "normal" activities, 90 percent of my time was still spent dealing with the worries I was creating about my health. When it was my turn to talk about what was happening in my life, my health felt like the most pressing topic to share.

"Do you remember me mentioning that I am taking part in a clinical drug trial?" I said, not looking at anyone in particular. "Well, I think that I am receiving the placebo treatment and I'm sensing that my lungs are continuing to decline. I'm also worried that the disease is progressing in my GI tract."

"Did your doctor tell you that you're not getting the medicine?" one of my friends asked.

"No, he doesn't know. Only the sponsors of the trial know in which group patients are placed."

I'll admit this was not the first time one of my updates started with some version of "The sky is falling!" For some friends or family members, I was probably starting to sound like Charlie Brown's teacher: "Wah, wah, who, wah, wah."

My friends kindly let me ramble for two or three minutes. Unfortunately, I was not paying attention to the verbal cues of the members of my audience. The tendency to ignore my listeners while talking was an observation that Eugene had once made note of. Had I been more attune to others on this evening, I may have seen what was coming next. Across the table, my friend Cathy seemed to be growing increasingly frustrated and impatient—or, at least, this is how I now interpret what was happening.

As I was mid-sentence, Cathy lifted herself slightly from her chair to grab her water glass and thrust it toward me while she screamed, "Donna! The glass isn't always half empty! Sometimes it is half full!"

Maybe it wasn't exactly a scream, but she raised the tone of her voice significantly. That, with the sudden move to push her glass, was enough to stop the show. My head lowered and my eyes looked down at the table. In an attempt to show her that I agreed, I mumbled, "Oh, yeah. Sure it is." For a brief moment, everyone at the table was quiet.

A sudden rush of familiar self-criticism flooded my head. *You're embarrassing yourself by talking about your health again. What a downer. Just shut up.*

Mercifully, someone spoke up and said something about the news or the weather or the ant crawling across the table. Cathy's abrupt outburst had me reeling, so I don't recall what was said. When our food came out of the kitchen soon after the interaction, we ate and chatted as if nothing had happened. For me, however, something had happened. I felt wounded, but I wasn't sure who wounded me. Cathy? Myself? Or both of us?

Cathy was a nurse by training. I always admired her can-do, check-it-off-the-list-and-move-on attitude. At another of our dinners, she casually revealed that she'd separated from her husband and had moved out of their family home. There'd been no indication before that there'd been a problem. She was the kind of person who just deals with the problem at hand and moves on. Her ability to face challenges head on, make decisions, and skip the self-doubt and rumination was enviable.

Our dinner on this evening was not the first time that Cathy had commented on my negativity. Once on a walk during a beach trip, she said to me, "You need to stop worrying." I chuckled and said, "You're right," as if I was grateful for receiving a new insight. Internally, however, I had heard it as judgment and scolded myself for being so negative. Cathy's delivery might be too forward for me, but I believed she was right. *I'm Debbie Downer Jr.*

At the restaurant, we finished our food and said our goodbyes at the front entrance. Once in the car, my self-loathing was suddenly replaced with anger. Instead of berating myself for being so pessimistic, I became furious at Cathy.

"Fuck you!" I said as I backed my car out of the parking lot next to the restaurant. I continued as part of my raging inner monologue, *Who does she think she is? I thought she was a nurse. Of all my friends, she should understand the level of uncertainty and danger I am facing.* As I took a breath, self-doubt crept back in. Maybe I was overreacting? After all, I was still living, still going out with friends, and still working. *But no! I'm not overreacting. I'm scared. Screw her!*

My phone rang. It was Jane.

"Hey, I wanted to check in to see how you're doing after Cathy's comment. I also wanted to apologize," she said.

"Apologize for what?" I was confused by her statement but grateful for her call.

"For not saying anything to support you in the moment."

I assured Jane that she didn't need to apologize. I hadn't expected her or anybody else to speak up, but it was helpful for me to know other's perspectives in case I was exaggerating the situation. A few days later, Laura called me as well. By the time she called, I had begun to understand that Cathy's reaction to me was a chance for me to discover more about who I was at this stage of my life journey. Unpacking this brief but significant occurrence felt crucial.

The first thing I realized was that I was not happy with my immediate response to Cathy's comment. I shut down and bought into her message that I was being too negative. I also learned that it felt good to be angry at Cathy, or anyone for that matter. I recognized that since my diagnosis, the only emotion I had been expressing was worry. I had not cried, nor had I thrown things across the room. I had not felt silly, happy, relieved, or astonished. I did have moments of feeling vulnerable, frightened, and annoyed, but a dose of anger was just what I needed.

If anxiety is as Eugene described—energy with no place to go—I found that anger was a way for that energy to finally escape my body. It had been stuffed down like a genie in a bottle. I would later uncover that rage and anger are not good places to be stuck, but at this moment, experiencing a strong emotion like anger felt good.

When I visited Eugene a couple of days after the friends' dinner, I told him about the situation with Cathy and how I reacted. His response was simple. "Why didn't you ask Cathy why she reacted the way she did?"

"Well, it was clear that she thought I was being negative and that she was tired of hearing me drone on about my worries."

"So, you know what she was thinking?" his voice was tinged with sarcasm.

"Well, I also didn't want to escalate the tension. We don't typically have conflict in this group."

"So, you know what she was thinking *and* you didn't think your friends could handle the tension if you asked Cathy about her response?" Eugene asked.

He didn't wait for my response. While I was considering his question, he said, "I'm noticing that you have a superpower."

"Here we go," I thought. Eugene had a way of making his points. I decided I would take the bait.

"What's my superpower?"

"You seem to know what people are thinking and feeling." Eugene smiled as I chuckled at his observation.

We both knew that, in reality, I did not know what others thought or felt. I made a lot of assumptions and told myself a lot of stories. Eugene's questions, however, were showing me just how frequently I did this now and during my entire life. Despite this insight, I continued to act as if I knew what other people were thinking or feeling.

The discussion about superpowers led me to consider what superpower I would want to have. I dropped out of the conversation with Eugene and turned my head toward the window over one of the sofas in his office. As I considered options, like the ability to fly, be invisible, or eat without gaining weight, I mentally crossed reading people's minds off my list. Interestingly, I never thought to add curing diseases to my list of options.

"Hello?" Eugene tried to get my attention back to our conversation.

"I was trying to identify which superpower I would like to have." I apologized for my momentary disengagement. "I'll have to think about it some more when I have a chance." I noticed that, again, I was planning to go back into my head for more thinking.

After time to reflect on the incident with my friends and on my conversation with Eugene, I've come to believe the following:

- I can say whatever I want to say about myself at a dinner with friends.
- Not everyone can or wants to handle another person's pain. They have their reasons. That they can't be an ear for me doesn't mean they aren't interested in helping me in other ways, such as helping me find a new doctor or helping me locate a special food that is more easily digested.
- Being more transparent about what I need from others is my job. If I need someone to listen as I vent for fifteen minutes, I need to let them know that's what I need. If I need advice, help, encouragement, or someone to agree that the situation sucks, I need to let them know.
- I should not forget to check in with others about what they want or need. While I may need to vent for fifteen minutes, they may only be able to listen to ten minutes of another person's sadness or pain. Agree to limits.

And finally, I have decided on the superpower I want to have. It's the superpower to accept. Accept what is. Accept who I am. Accept others as they are.

CHAPTER 12.

Do You Have Any Questions for Me?

———

One week, I made the mistake of arriving to my appointment with Eugene without a topic to discuss.

After I arrived, we exchanged greetings and I sat in the wooden rocking chair, my usual spot for our discussions. I sat quietly. Suddenly the silence felt awkward. "I don't have anything to talk about," I admitted.

When I worked with other counselors earlier in life, I started the sessions by giving an account of what had happened since the last visit. "On Monday this happened and he said, then on Tuesday, I had a meeting and she said . . ." I didn't expect that I would have any great insights from these conversations. I used my time with counselors to clear my head and to air my complaints.

Eugene's counseling method was different from that of other counselors. He admitted to me that while he was aware of the importance of people sharing significant life events, he was not especially interested in specific events. It didn't matter to him who had annoyed me or what had happened in my childhood. He was more curious about how I handled those situations now.

"It doesn't matter to me if you're mad at Jesus or your father or your coworker. None of them are sitting in the office with us," he would say.

Years of conditioning left me without knowing any other way to start our sessions. Often, I just launched into a description of an event from my week and he would skillfully turn my comments into a rich discussion about how I didn't look people in the eye when I was talking with them or about how I was passive aggressive and I should accept that about myself (both insights are true and I own that I'm not in the mood to work on these behaviors).

On this particular day, the week's doctor visits, work meetings, and family squabbles didn't seem important. Nothing was floating around in my head that I wanted to talk about. Perhaps I should have seen this as a sign of progress. After a few years of nonstop intrusive thoughts, I was suddenly empty-headed. Unfortunately, the potential significance of the moment was lost on me. Instead, I frantically tried to call up a situation worthy of a therapy conversation. *After all*, I thought, *I'm paying for the session. I should talk about something.*

Eugene leaned back in his office chair, and before I could identify the worst thing that had happened to me that week—my usual mode of operation—he responded to my declaration of not having anything to talk about.

"Okay," he began. "Then is there anything that you want to ask me?"

By now, I should have known that if I was not talking, he would take us down a mystery road—mystery to me, that is. Perhaps he knew what road we were about to go down, but it was never clear that he had a plan when he started a conversation with a question.

As I looked down at my feet to avoid his gaze, I noticed that my socks didn't match. I lifted my head to look at Eugene. He was staring at me, waiting for an answer. As the seconds ticked by, I recognized that I was in my head, trying to process what he was asking. *How should I answer this question?* I wondered, also reminding myself to self-edit. My answer, I knew, should not include any of the language he would challenge, including his off-limit words.

During our session the week prior, Eugene suggested I start noticing more about the people I was with and what they were doing and saying. This was part of his effort to help me pay more attention to what was in front of me. When he asked if I wanted to ask him any questions, I did not make a connection to this earlier discussion.

I admit, I was a head traveler. So much time was spent in my head that even when I was in conversation with another person, I missed a lot of what was happening in front of me. For example, I seldom noticed differences in how someone looked when I saw them. They would need to dye their hair neon green for me to say, "Something is different about you. Hm. What is it? Oh, your hair!" Instead of paying attention, I was trying to identify what I was going to say. I was not fully present. But not noticing someone's physical changes was one thing; not hearing what they are saying was another.

"You need to be more curious," Eugene advised. This was not the first time he had said that. I jotted it down in my journal in hopes that the notation would remind me of this frequent insight.

"I'm trying to be more present," I said, ignoring his disdain for the word *try*.

"You are always present," he said, meaning that as long as a person is breathing, they are present. He followed his declaration with advice. "You need to be more *aware*."

I agreed with him that I needed to be more aware and more curious, but other than nodding in agreement, I wondered what to say. I felt like I should drop my pencil on the floor so the teacher would avoid calling on me to answer the question that had been posed. Eugene sat looking in my direction, seemingly unfazed by the tension filling the room.

Replaying his words in my mind, I told myself that he had just issued a challenge for me to pay attention to what was in front of me in that moment, right there in his office. But what exactly was I supposed to look at? I wasn't in the middle of Times Square, New York City or the National Orchid Garden of Singapore, two rich playgrounds for the senses. We were just sitting in his undecorated office.

I accepted the challenge. Why not?

Rotating my head to scan the room. I observed my environment as if I were a witness to an event that would have to be explained to the police. Eugene was sitting in his black office chair, both feet on the ground. I noticed he was impeccably groomed and styled. The tone of his skin was light brown. He was clean shaven on his face and sporting a bald-head look. He wore business casual clothing—on this day, a maroon-colored, polo-type short-sleeved shirt buttoned at the neck. His slacks were a charcoal denim, belted with a black belt. He didn't wear a tie or jacket, but on other occasions I had seen him in a sweater. His personal styling choices were in stark contrast to the furnishing of his office, which to me had the charm of a cheap hotel room in a war-torn country.

While the discussion switched to a different subject after my quick scan of Eugene and his workspace, I was aware that I had gained a few lessons through the brief exercise. The more you pay attention in the moment, the more you will see and the more you will be able to enjoy it. I also noted that sight was the only one of my senses I used to be aware, and I didn't focus on myself or how I was feeling during the exercise. I needed to do some more work on being more aware, including learning to be more curious.

I was not thinking about the previous week's discussion or the lessons learned when he posed the question, "Is there anything you want to ask me?"

After what seemed like five minutes but was probably thirty seconds, I finally answered his question. "I'm not sure."

His question made me feel surprisingly uneasy and I didn't know why. Something about the way Eugene asked the question made me think he wasn't looking for the same kind of response other health care providers seek when they ask, "Do you have any questions for me?" When my doctors ask this question, I assume they are asking if I want to know more about my health concern or about the treatment plan.

With my personal medical notebook in hand, I'm always prepared to ask plenty of questions at doctor visits. Remarkably, however, I had never thought to ask Eugene any questions. Maybe on my first visit I asked him if he had experience treating people with serious medical illnesses? I don't recall. But on this visit, I felt he wasn't asking me if I had any treatment-related questions. I believed he was asking me if I wanted to know about him as a person. At this point, months into our work together, I knew very little about him as a person.

Some time was needed to process my uneasiness and consider how I would respond if the topic came up again, which I felt sure it would. I surmised that Eugene would recognize I was evading his question and want to know why. Somehow I skirted the question, however, moving our conversation on to something else. Eugene didn't push for more.

After our session, I went to the coffee shop down the street, ordered my usual beverage of choice, an earl grey vanilla tea latte, and sat at my favorite table in the middle of the bustle.

I opened my journal, which I called my Eugene Journal or E-journal for short, to write a list of questions I might ask Eugene. What did I want to know about him?

With pen in hand, I jotted down the questions that came to me in that moment.

Are you trained to treat people who are facing death?
Do you have the skills to help me grow?
What is your academic background?
What was your family like?
What are your hobbies?
What are your political views?
What brings you joy?
Why did you go into this line of work?

Steam rose from my cup as I sipped the tea latte and looked up from my list of questions. I saw two women talking about a real estate opportunity, a student seated at the table against the wall writing a course paper on his computer, and two old friends who had bumped into each other at the milk and sugar station exchanging news about their children. At least, these were the stories I told myself to divert my attention away from the task at hand. As I made up stories about other people's lives, I realized why I was afraid to ask Eugene personal questions.

First, I thought that by asking him questions I was crossing a professional boundary, like asking your doctor, lawyer, or plumber, "What's your home address?" I also recognized that I was conflicted about using counseling time I was paying for to discuss anything other than me. And the last and scariest reason was that I did not know what I would do if I found out that his views of the world were wildly different than mine.

This brief moment of reflection in the coffee shop was interesting. However, I was still unsure what question, if any, I would ask Eugene if the opportunity presented itself again.

On my next visit, Eugene opened the conversation with another intriguing question. "Do you make friends easily?"

In response, I jokingly said, "I really must come to these visits more prepared, or at least with an agenda of what I want to talk about." Eugene laughed, but his question still hung in the air.

I had plenty of friends, including friends I kept in touch with from grade school and college. I had friends from my book club and from my old running group. I had friends from work and from the connections I made while my children were in school. Many of my friends had supported me through the ups and downs of life and continued to support me as I dealt with my health crisis. But to answer Eugene's specific question, I said, "No, I don't make friends easily."

As usual, I didn't quite understand where he was going with this question, but it led me to think about my friendships.

"I don't need more friends," I said a bit defensively. "If anything, I just need to nurture my existing friendships."

How many of my friends saw the full me? How many have let me see the full them? I wanted at least some of my friendships to have depth. I wanted to be able to cry without embarrassment in front of these friends, fart or vomit in front of them, or be angry in front of them. I also wanted them to feel they could do these things in front of me without embarrassment or without fear of abandonment.

"I want to be authentic," I said.

"You don't think that you are being authentic with others?" Eugene asked with a quizzical look.

"I think that I only show part of myself."

"When someone is not authentic," Eugene stated, "they are not accepting part of themselves. What are you not accepting?"

His question lingered as I waited for an answer to pop into my brain. I found myself interpreting the question as, "What are you hiding?"

The first thought that came to me was related to my illnesses. It felt safe to say I had not totally accepted them. This lack of acceptance kept me from telling most of my colleagues about what I had been experiencing since my diagnoses. But I also hid other parts of me, like my immature and distasteful side. I reasoned that since Eugene had been exposed to the dark and warped parts of my mind, he could also handle other parts of my true self. Despite that belief, I was hesitant to share what I was thinking.

He stared at me in an effort to get me to answer his question. Somewhat humiliated but also determined to tell him what had popped into my mind, I finally just blurted out, "I react in a childish manner to scatological humor." I tried to balance my immaturity with the big word.

In response to the unveiling of my secret, he asked, "That's what you're hiding and not accepting about yourself?"

"Yes," I said and decided to continue, "I basically laugh so hard that I end up crying and snorting whenever I hear any fart or poop story." At the time, I didn't quite know why I was sharing this with Eugene. All I knew is that I felt some shame over this personality quirk unless I was with my siblings, who shared the same quirk. For all I knew, Eugene was probably disappointed that I didn't tell him I was a serial killer, but I didn't know what he felt because I didn't look at him or ask him.

Despite my embarrassment, I continued by telling him a story about the time I worked as a surgery assistant for a very stoic and professional doctor. He removed skin cancers using a multi-step surgical procedure. On one occasion, an elderly patient repeatedly farted while she was on the surgery table undergoing the first step in the procedure. "Let's finish this before she kills us," the doctor said to me after bandaging her and sending her to the waiting area to await the next step in the procedure. Needless to say, I had considerable difficulty keeping myself together as we continued with her remaining treatment.

My eyes filled with tears and I started to belly laugh as I told Eugene this story. I chastised myself; *Why did you just embarrass yourself with such a classless story?*

Then Eugene, a consummate professional, said, "And what are you feeling right now?"

Oddly, the belly laugh felt cathartic. Sure, I felt ashamed, but I also recognized that I had been authentic. The point wasn't that I wanted to start telling fart jokes to my friends and colleagues, but that I wanted to be able to be myself even when parts of me are not so pretty or proper. The last chapters of life can be revealing and messy. I noticed that holding back parts of me was starting to take a lot of energy. And energy was starting to be in short supply.

The conversations with Eugene during these three consecutive sessions led me to realize I wanted to work on how I interact with the people in my life. I needed to become more aware, curious, and authentic. Being curious and aware were good places to start. I'll work on being more authentic later. I decided to add a new goal to my list of therapy goals.

I want to strengthen my relationships by asking questions and by paying attention when I am with others, I wrote in my E-journal.

My next visit with Eugene felt like a good time to tell him why I had been hesitant to ask him questions during our prior visits and to tell him that I believe it is important for me to use our time together to learn how to build stronger relationships with others.

I started with him.

"I wonder if I could ask you a question?" He smiled in assent so I proceeded to ask something I'd been eager to know. "Do you have children?"

CHAPTER 13.

Ben & Jerry's

———

Not many people outside of my family know my secret addiction: ice cream.

Coffee ice cream is my favorite, followed by chocolate, strawberry, fudge swirl, mint chocolate chip—any flavor, to be honest. There's no better gift for me than a gift card to Cold Stone Creamery.

My passion for ice cream has become a family story that everyone but me thinks is funny. One morning when my sons were very young, one of them caught me with "my hand in the cookie jar." Actually, the way he told the story at age five or six was, "Last night, I crept downstairs and saw mom eating all of the ice cream with a spoon, right out of the box." At the time, I was embarrassed that my sugary addiction and my poor dining habits were being exposed, but with the goal of accepting who I am, I can now proudly declare that I am a middle-of-the-night, straight-out-of-the-tub ice cream lover! Or, I was. I can't eat late at night now because of my scleroderma-related GI issues, but I'd do it during the day now that my kids are off in college, Tums by my side.

Eugene didn't know this when he one day gave me a new assignment. I was to go to a shopping center in town, sit in the picnic area outside of the Ben & Jerry's ice cream shop, and people-watch. That is, I was to sit at a table or on the grass, be curious, and use my senses to pay attention to everything around me. I knew what he wanted from me, but when he gave me the assignment, all I could focus on was the fact that I had a reason other than gluttony to go to Ben & Jerry's. I thought, *I should get an ice cream cone while I'm there. I need to have a believable cover story for my lingering.*

The assignment grew out of several conversations we'd had about travel, specifically international travel. The list of countries Eugene had visited was impressive. At some point, he was hoping to add Antarctica to his list. I also enjoyed travel to other countries, which is a more widely known fact about me than my passion for ice cream. Even my doctors knew it was important to me. All three of the doctors I consider most important to my care would ask where I had been or where I was going even before they asked how I was feeling. Talking about trips was the litmus test of my well-being. If I wasn't willing to engage in a conversation about an upcoming or recent trip, they knew that something was wrong.

When Eugene assigned me to sit outside of Ben & Jerry's, my son and I were planning a trip to Vietnam. I wanted to expose him to a faraway culture, but I also wanted to go to a country that was warm, flat, and far—warm so I didn't have to deal with Raynaud's symptoms, flat so I didn't have to worry about my ability to breath in high altitudes, and far because I wanted to be sure I took those long-haul trips before I couldn't. My husband shot down my ideas for other locations due to safety concerns but was fine with me taking our son to Vietnam. That worked for me.

While I loved to talk about my trips, my internal voice told me that my conversations about travel were awkward and confusing. When discussing my trip to Vietnam with Eugene, for instance, one minute I told him I was planning to float down the Mekong River in a flat-bottomed, wooden sampan boat while wearing a conical rice hat, and the next minute, with tears in my eyes, I told him that I thought my lungs were becoming cement blocks and soon I wouldn't be able to breathe. I was animated and full of energy with one sentence and morose and weepy with the next one.

Eugene understood that some people compartmentalize so at times it seems as if they lead two lives. An example of this might be a friend privately sharing that they hate their husband and are thinking of a divorce and then revealing an upcoming trip to Paris to celebrate their anniversary. While processing the painful side of their lives, they also go on living. People are complex, but the fact that I could talk about travel and death in the same sentence felt disingenuous, or at least hypochondriacal.

"Will others understand that I can be very sick while also be able to travel?" I asked, though I should have known his answer.

"Does it matter what they think?"

It did matter to me what people thought, but I'm not sure why. I wrote in my journal several times over the years, *How do I want people to view me? Why do I want them to see me as sick sometimes and not sick other times?* My internal struggle over this issue came out in nightmares. I was fighting with people who assumed I was not sick, only for me to then show them I was sick.

Several times, I dreamed I had gone to the grocery store and parked in the accessible parking spot. I walked unaided into the store, shopped all of the aisles, but then was too tired to carry my bags to my car. As I exited the store with a helper, a woman loudly announced that I should leave the handicap parking spots to those who needed them, presumably those using wheel chairs. As my dream continued, I suddenly saw myself dragging an oxygen tank behind me and wearing a nasal cannula in my nostrils.

I imagined that people thought I was making shit up, or that perhaps my real illness was Munchausen's syndrome, the mental health illness characterized by people acting sick when they are not in order to garner sympathy. The truth was that I had invisible illnesses. Managing my various symptoms was one full-time job and managing the constant chatter in my head was another. The only vacation I got from both of these jobs was when I went on a trip.

Traveling offered plenty of distractions. While away, I paid attention to the sights, sounds, and smells of the new places and I didn't dwell on my breathing, doctor visits, medical tests, or fights with insurance. I thought, *If I could only learn how to feel this way at home.*

On the day I told Eugene I was planning a trip to Vietnam, I mentioned why I wanted to travel to places like South Korea,

Australia, New Zealand, Thailand, and Singapore. I said that I kept thinking, *My world is getting smaller. Soon I will be unable to leave the country, the state, the house, and ultimately, my bed. My travel days are very limited.* By now, I knew I was creating future horror stories and I was not focused on the present moment. However, I also knew my thoughts were still scaring me.

In response to me sharing these thoughts with Eugene, he reminded me, "You do not have a crystal ball. No one does. You may or may not lose the ability to travel." Neither of us knew at the time what was in store for all of us in the year 2020.

Everyone loses the ability to travel at some point in their lives—except Eugene, who is like the man in the book *The 100-Year-Old Man Who Climbed Out the Window and Disappeared* by Jonas Jonasson. In this story, a hundred-year-old man goes on his last adventure after a lifetime of getting tangled up in the biggest historical events around the world. I would like to believe I have many more years to travel, and perhaps I do. If and when my world does shrink, I want two things to be true. First, I want to know I traveled as long as I could; second, I want to accept and find joy in whatever is in front of me. Eugene taught me that I make myself happy when I travel. When I am at home, I also want to make myself happy.

"Let's explore this," Eugene said. "What do you think is going on? Why do you think travel is so important to you?"

"I don't know," I said at first, then continued sharing my thoughts out loud. "For some reason, I would describe a day sitting in a coffee shop in Paris or Timbuktu as the best day ever but would describe a day in a local coffee shop in Greensboro as an epic waste of time." I further described how in another country, I might watch how a woman feeds her child or I might observe how a group of men interact over a midday coffee. "I would never sit long enough to observe those things at home," I said.

"So you are not curious about people here?" he asked.

"Not really." Perhaps I sounded a bit arrogant to believe I already knew and understood the people in my community. I assumed that I knew how they fed their children and what they were talking about during midday coffee breaks. Recall, I do have a superpower!

Eugene decided to repeat my absurd statement for emphasis.

"You already know all there is to know about our city." He smiled wryly. "Have you been to the burial site of the Buffalo Soldiers off of Asheboro Street and Martin Luther King Drive?"

"Well, no," I said, mentally revising my previous remark. "Maybe I don't know everything, but I've never really wanted to learn." I was shocked by the words I heard myself say. It was time to learn how to be curious no matter where I was.

Due to weather and other inconveniences, it took me six months to complete my Ben & Jerry's assignment. That didn't stop me from enjoying some ice cream though. I went to other ice cream shops to satisfy my cravings, but those visits did not count toward completion of my assignment. The delay also didn't stop me from practicing "going to my senses" and being more aware in other situations, like when I went out to eat. It would be a while before I understood that I didn't need to leave my house to practice being aware of what was in front of me.

Not long after my discussion with Eugene, I went to lunch with a friend at a new Thai restaurant. Thai food happens to be my favorite type of food next to ice cream, so I was excited for the treat and the opportunity to see this friend. We met at the front of the restaurant and were escorted to a table for two. After general greetings of "you look so great" and "what nice weather we're having," she asked me how I was doing. At that moment, I felt great. Somehow, I almost always felt okay while meeting with friends or family members, a testament to the power of social interactions.

"My therapist is helping me become more aware of what is in front of me," I said, realizing this was an opportunity to practice. As I spoke, I scanned our environment.

Paying attention, I noticed her beautiful pastel-colored blouse, the window behind her chair, and the people sitting on either side of us. On our table for two, I suddenly noticed a small but lovely floral arrangement in a vase next to an assortment of condiments. Colorful and fragrant, I smiled and pointed it out to my friend.

"This is an example of what I've been missing when I'm thinking about the future instead of paying attention to the now." We both smiled and made note of the benefits of paying attention to the moment.

Another opportunity to practice occurred the day after my friend lunch. Scheduled for another medical test, I could feel the rising anxiety as I drove to the clinic. My heart beat faster and I became aware I was having trouble controlling intrusive thoughts. They weren't even complete thoughts, just fragments I interpreted to mean, "I'm so worried. I'm so worried." To ward off a complete panic attack, I shouted an order as if I were a general in an army: "Go to your senses!" While still driving, I started verbalizing what I was seeing. "I see a yellow sign. I see a line in the middle of the road. I see a gray car exiting off the road to the right. I see trees. I see dead leaves." Dead leaves? This image stopped my visual exercise. I believed that by becoming more aware of the world around me, I would see things that made me happy, like beautiful flowers.

"What's the purpose of going to my senses if I'm seeing dead leaves?" The experience left me confused. Later, I told Eugene I was confused about the benefit of going to my senses if I experienced things that were unpleasant, like dead leaves.

"Dead leaves are necessary for new leaves to grow," he responded.

My internal self shook my head and said, *That's such a Eugene statement.*

Finally, I made my way to Ben & Jerry's to complete my original assignment of paying attention and being curious. I paid my respects to the local ice cream shop by buying a single-scoop sugar cone with Coffee Coffee BuzzBuzzBuzz ice cream. After grabbing a few napkins, I exited the shop and sat at one of the small, round metal tables for guests. The afternoon was a comfortable seventy-two degrees at 1:00 p.m. Only one other guest sat nearby, a woman with a baby stroller at the end of the large bricked patio area on the other side of the four-tiered, circular water fountain. While I waited to see if other people would gather in the area, I paid attention to my purchase. I savored the last few licks of the melting ice cream and then enjoyed the crispy bites of the sugar cone—delicious! When I finished, I looked around but found I had little curiosity for the mom and baby in the distance, and I didn't see any other people. I was also void of any interest in the other businesses around the public sitting area. *Did I just fail the assignment?* I wondered.

Despite being surprised by the floral arrangement at the restaurant and the wonderful flavors and textures of my ice cream cone, I still struggled with the why and how of being curious and attentive. My attempts to practice did not always give me the same amount of joy I felt while sitting at a coffee shop in Lisbon, Portugal, or Addis Ababa in Ethiopia (where, really, they have the best coffee.) *I need to think about this some more*, I thought, not recognizing that again I had gone back into my head, no longer paying attention to the present.

Eugene once said to me, "You're always living in the world. You're just paying attention to what is in your head oppose to what is in front of you." Sixty years of not paying attention was not going to change in a few months or even a few years. I was very determined, however, to learn to appreciate whatever was in front of me wherever I was, before my world got any smaller. I needed more practice.

In the meantime, pass the ice cream scooper or just give me the box and a spoon.

CHAPTER 14.

Time Well Spent

It seems a bit late to be looking for your life's purpose when you are entering the last chapter of your life, but by November 2017, two years after my diagnosis, here I was. I suddenly felt this overwhelming need to figure out what my purpose was so I could "live life to its fullest." By doing this, I felt sure I could lie in my deathbed at peace, with no regrets.

First, I acknowledge that I spent more time than one should on what it would be like lying on your death bed. I can assure you, however, that the end of life was not something I gave much thought prior to my diagnoses. Like many people, I knew I would die. We all will. But I believed I had years and years before I had to face that stage of life, and that when it came I would beg death to take me. Many people wish for a long life, but the thought of reaching a hundred years old—a birthday my grandmother was able to celebrate—made me cringe. No thank you. However, if treatments are found for arthritis, memory loss, and the rest of aging issues, I would reconsider.

"Are you afraid of death?" Eugene asked me a few times while we worked together. I never hesitated to answer.

"No. I am not afraid of being dead." I did not want my kids to grow up without a mother, but I wasn't actually afraid of being dead.

I imagine there are some benefits to being dead. Being dead may allow you to come back to life in some better form, like a dog. It may provide you an opportunity to watch the lives of others without having to worry or get involved. Some people believe that when a loved one passes, they're in a better place or aren't suffering anymore. Others don't fear death because they're convinced that they will meet their spiritual leader. When my husband's grandmother died at age one hundred and five, I recall feeling joy because I knew she believed she was on her way to meet Jesus. Some people also believe that in death they will meet other loved ones who have already passed, such as parents, friends, or cherished pets.

While all of these beliefs may be possible, I find myself particularly drawn to what Anne Lamott wrote about death in her beautiful book *Bird by Bird*. A friend who was facing her own mortality and was struggling with the thought of leaving her two-year-old child asked Anne to share the silver lining to death. Anne responded, "You're not going to have to see any more naked pregnant pictures of Demi Moore," referring to a recent magazine cover of the actress (1994, 135). I can think of a few things I also will not mind letting go.

For me, death means not having to hear another word about the Kardashians or any upcoming elections. Worrying about my thinning hair, expanding waistline, and sagging breasts will also be a thing of the past. Some days, I think death would be preferable to seeing or hearing about all of the corrupt politicians, but I'm not really there yet. I'd like to live long enough to see their final chapters play out.

The thought of hugging my mother and father again or seeing my freshman college roommate make me smile. And having a worry-free or a pain-free existence also sounds nice. However, these are not the reasons I don't fear death. The top reason I don't fear death is that I have created the belief that when I die, I will have access to the answers for all of life's questions. What could be more thrilling than knowing everything?

If this belief is true, then I would finally learn the answers to so many questions. Who killed JonBenét Ramsey? What causes scleroderma? How big is space? What governmental structure is the best? Is there a God? How often did my sister steal clothes out of my closet when we were growing up?

On the occasions when Eugene asked me if I feared death, my full answer to his question was, "I don't fear death, but I do fear getting there."

I fear the suffering that often accompanies the process of dying. Scleroderma doesn't typically let people ease out of life like a sunset. For some people, scleroderma and the medications they must take create significant pain and discomfort. Even now as I type this paragraph, my intestines feel uneasy and my feet feel the pain of someone who is walking barefoot in the Maine snow. Many people with scleroderma also have pain associated with inflamed and contracted joints, or pain from a dysfunctional gastrointestinal system. Scleroderma does not have the monopoly on pain, however. Dying from any disease or even old age can be physically torturous.

The possibilities of physical pain and suffering on the way to death still worried me, but entering my third year of facing my own mortality, I began distressing myself about another potential end of life concern: regret.

If you google "deathbed regrets" (and why would you?), you find lists of things people say they regret when they are facing death. Some of the top regrets heard from dying patients are:

1. They lived the life others expected rather than living their own truth
2. They worked too hard
3. They didn't have the courage to express their true feelings
4. They lost touch with friends
5. They didn't allow themselves to be happier

In his memoir, *When Breath Becomes Air*, author Paul Kalanithi raised another question that many people consider during the last stage of life: "What do I do with my time now?" While juggling a career as a physician and as a new father with a lung cancer diagnosis, he reflected, "If only I knew how many months or years I had left. Tell me three months, I'd spend time with family. Tell me one year, I'd write a book. Give me ten years, I'd get back to treating diseases" (2016, 161).

This statement resonated with me. I thought, *If only I knew how long I had left, I could prioritize and plan my time.*

My own discovery process of how I wanted to live my life going forward took several months. I found a vintage photo album, thirteen inches by fifteen inches in size, in a pile of items I had set aside for either the trash or Goodwill. The album had heavy stock paper pages, thick enough to bare the weight of taped photographs, ticket stubs, and birthday cards. My sons and I had glued a few space-related news stories to some of the pages, such as a story on how space toilets work and a story on the Hubble Space Telescope, but most of the pages remained blank. I decided to use the album as a tool for a self-directed visioning project.

My first goal was to figure out what question or questions I wanted to answer through this exercise. On the first blank page in the album, I jotted down a list of questions.

What is my vision and mission?

- What are my values?
- What is my purpose?
- What is my legacy?
- What is my personal brand?
- Why am I here? Why do I exist?
- What should I be doing with my time that feels important?
- What can I do to change the world or make a difference?

Considering each question, I realized I didn't want to brand myself or find my purpose. Generally, I wanted to make a difference in the world, but this goal felt too big and overwhelming. I was thankful for just getting out of bed. I don't think I had it in me to focus on changing the world. Reflecting a bit longer on my list, the question I needed to answer found me: How do I want to spend the time I have so, in the end, when I'm lying in my deathbed, I will say my time was well spent?

When I visited Eugene around this time, I told him I had an overwhelming need to figure out what to do with my time. I said, "I'm struggling with thoughts that are saying I have to find happiness." I had started to notice that I was jealous of friends who knew how to spend their time. They were planning trips and filling their calendars with various life activities. I believed there was something I was not doing that needed to be done before I died—not a bucket list exactly. Searching for the right words, I said, "I just can't pinpoint what I should be doing."

In response to my rambling, Eugene said, "There is no 'should.'" This was another off-limit word. He continued, "You are doing exactly what you want with your time. We are all doing exactly what we want with our time."

Having to accept that sitting on the sofa playing Solitaire on my phone with *Dateline* playing on TV was what I really wanted to be doing all day was hard—but, dammit, he was right. I was doing what I wanted to do at that moment, but I wished I wanted to do something else. I felt it was time to move on to other activities. I no longer wanted to spend my time this way.

"Donna always did what she wanted to do," I asked Eugene to say when my time came. He agreed to say this in my eulogy as long as he could also say I was dictating what he should say. I agreed and we smiled knowing control was still a bit of an issue. I own it.

Continuing to search for the answer to my question of how to spend my time, I opened the photo album and wrote a question at the top of each page.

When do I feel most at peace (calm, with no anxiety)?

- When have I cried out of joy, amazement, or silliness?
- What are my values? How do I spend my time? What do I want to do more of?
- When have I felt the most fulfilled? When I have been most proud of myself?
- What does taking care of myself look like?
- What kinds of hobbies do I like? What do I like?
- What don't I like?
- If my mind were a room, how would I renovate the room to be one I enjoyed visiting?
- How do I want to be remembered?
- What things or activities have others done that I admire?
- If I had a bucket list, what would be on it?

When inspired, I took various colored markers and scribbled over each page. Back and forth, I jumped question to question. It did not need to be a linear process.

The exercise took months, and while most of the time it was a solo activity, sometimes I dragged friends in to join me. On several occasions, for instance, I met with a friend over coffee to discuss some of these questions. While at the beach with another friend, we cut images from magazines to make vision boards. We never actually made complete boards, but I found that the fifteen to twenty images I clipped from the magazines aligned perfectly with what I had scribbled in the pages of my album.

When I shared my reflective progress with Eugene, he asked, "Are you going toward something or away from something?" I wasn't sure but wondered, *Does it matter?*

"I just want to get off of the sofa and stop wasting my time," I ended up saying.

"Are you wasting your time?'" he asked. "Perhaps you need to stop judging and accept what is."

"I don't want 'couch-sitter' to be what is!" I said emphatically.

"You must want it. That is where you are. You're on the sofa. Why is that where you want to be?"

His question swirled in my head. *Why am I on the couch so much?* I asked myself. After what felt like a full minute, I responded, "I'm there because I'm tired or because I don't feel well. I just want to sit and recover or feel better."

Eugene followed by saying, "There are plenty of people who would love to have time to sit on the sofa and take care of themselves. Maybe you could become the 'best couch-sitter' one could be?"

Our conversation seemed silly, but it resulted in huge insights for me, not unlike many of our other discussions. In my E-journal that day, I scribbled, "I am the best couch-sitter there is—or at least in Greensboro, NC."

The visioning process helped me understand that I didn't need to form a new start-up company or solve world hunger to be a peace. I learned that each moment, I'm doing exactly what I want to be doing, and if it is sitting on the sofa, then so be it. I don't need to run away from what I've been doing, but there are other things I want to run toward more often. These are:

Nature

- Art, music, dance, and creativity
- Writing
- Travel

Organization, like organizing my personal accounts and belongings

While I can, I'd like to focus on getting out of bed to enjoy these things instead of obsessing about being in my deathbed.

CHAPTER 15.

The Imaginary Toolbox

Every day, I experience at least one moment of panic. It starts by me gasping for extra breaths of air. Then, my heart rate speeds up and I find myself listening to a repeating loop of terrifying thoughts.

Most often, these moments are just that: a moment, maybe a few seconds. They may be triggered by the thought of an upcoming medical test, a quick movement that leaves me searching for an extra breath, or a sudden realization that I can no longer do a certain thing I did last week. Moments of panic may also occur for no apparent reason at all. Now I am quicker to recover, but in the first couple of years after my scleroderma and lung disease diagnoses, panic subsided slowly.

One night, I awoke to a troubling amount of post-nasal drip. In North Carolina where spring pollen covers everything, almost everyone suffers from seasonal allergies and post-nasal drip, at least for a couple of months. On this particular night, I could not swallow the mucous fast enough. My inner voice started speaking to me, dredging up again the metaphor used by my first gastroenterologist. *Your esophagus has become a lead pipe!* My chest tightened and panic grew. *Could I actually drown myself?* I wondered as I conjured up an image of what it would be like to drown in your own fluids. Ultimately, I was able to resolve the nasal drip and calm my thoughts, but it was a difficult night.

Progressive, incurable diseases like mine provide ample opportunities for people with anxiety to create panic. Fortunately, through my work with Eugene, I started to collect a whole toolbox of coping skills and activities that could help me resolve or get through these times with a lot less suffering.

I had no tools in my toolbox early on, or maybe I had some but they were ineffective in my current situation. We all find ways to deal with the stressors in life. A friend, for example, jokingly says that the only tool for anxiety and panic in her toolbox is alcohol. A lot of people use this tool to get through crises or challenges while others use distractions like gambling, spending money, sleeping, or watching endless TV. These strategies may be destructive if overused and, fortunately, they don't appeal to me—with the exception of watching endless TV.

Other than watching TV, the way I most often dealt with stress in the past was sitting paralyzed in my thoughts until someone or something distracted me. Distraction is still a helpful tool, but counting on external saviors as my only tool was not going to resolve every bout of anxiety, panic, and depression. I needed more strategies and tools.

Tools are any action I can take or any question I can ask myself that will help me break the cycle of despair or worry I have created. One of the first tools I put in my imaginary anxiety toolbox came from an early conversation with Eugene.

The first Christmas after my diagnoses had just passed. I walked into Eugene's office, heaped my coat, purse, and backpack on top of one of his sofas, and took a seat. I knew I needed to talk about the heavy and dark feelings I had carried through the holiday season. After an exchange of New Year's greetings, I said, "I've been having a pity party for myself."

"Was it fun?" Eugene asked, seeking more information about the fictitious event.

Fighting the emotion starting to show in my face, I replied, "No."

"It seems if you're going to throw yourself a party, it ought to be *fun*!"

We sat quietly while I processed his clever play on words. Then he broke the silence by adding, "Why did you want to have a pity party?"

The question didn't sit so well with me at the time. "I didn't!" I responded with a hint of irritation.

"But you did," he said. "You had one."

I blindly stared out the window over the sofa to the right of me. Momentarily forgetting I was in conversation with Eugene, I paid attention to the thoughts popping into my head. *I don't want to be depressed and think, "woe is me."*

What is he talking about? Finally, I responded to his statement. "I threw myself a pity party because what I really want is to have a big, big cry!"

"You can cry here," he said compassionately.

His words went straight to my heart. Tears welled up in my eyes, but I fought the intense desire to cry. Normally, I wasn't much of a crier, but I had become even more resistant to the act of crying. The stuffy nose that goes along with crying makes breathing difficult. In addition, successful nose blowing requires that one be able to blow air. These realities make crying more challenging for people in my situation. I swallowed the huge lump in my throat and successfully held back a complete melt down. The exchange meant a lot to me. I felt like he cared.

Not long after our conversation, I vowed to dance each time I caught myself having a pity party. Somehow the toe tapping and bum wiggling lifts the feelings of despair in the moment. Pity party jigs became one of my first tools for accepting what is. I now accept that I throw pity parties. When I recognize that I am having one, I make it fun! (You're invited to my next one. Please bring your dancing shoes.)

In addition to asking me questions, Eugene often told stories to make a point. During one visit, I announced, "I'm always mad." This statement provided an entry way into a lesson about how one can deal with poor drivers. The lesson led me to another useful panic-busting tool.

"Why are you doing this to yourself?" he asked in response to my comment about feeling mad. His assertion that I needed to own my response to events was still new to me at the time of this visit. To make his point, he continued with a story about dealing with road-rage: "The person driving poorly next to you is not pissing you off. You're pissing you off. Instead of creating rage within yourself when you encounter a poor driver, practice a new reaction."

"What do you mean?" I asked, truly interested in the magic he might pull out of his hat. Eugene had an ability to take a simple topic and shock you with an unexpected twist.

"Well," he started, "You could pull the bad driver over and give them a lecture. You could drive to the police station and turn in the person's license plate number, or you could write a book about how to drive."

"Or," he added as if he needed one more suggestion, "you could just be curious." Seeing the look of confusion on my face, he elaborated on the idea by saying I could wonder where the person was going to or coming from.

To this suggestion, I thought, *Hm, no. I don't care about that. On the other hand, I might be curious to know why the person is driving like an asshole.*

After this conversation, I shared Eugene's wisdom with my sister. We both particularly liked his suggestion that one could write a book about frustrating situations. We ignored his other messages about taking ownership for the anger we generate or about being more curious than frustrated. "What are you going to do, write a book about it?" became the go-to mantra when my sister and I talked about life's frustrations.

My sister lived about nine hundred miles away from me in a town not far from our childhood home. She was the one I called, particularly since our mom had passed, with the boring tidbits of life. One night while chatting on the phone with her, I started to complain about a very minor yet annoying situation I experienced in a waiting area of an airport during the delay of a red-eye flight.

"Parents sitting next to me kept giving their toddler a super-sized soft drink and then repeatedly swatted him when he wouldn't stay in his chair," I droned on without concern for the assumptions I was making about who these people were and what they were giving the child to drink.

Of course, how this child was being parented at 1:00 a.m. in an airport was none of my business, and the fact that I was becoming irritated highlighted both my own inability to deal with minor frustrations and my learned behavior of judging other people. After I told my sister about the incident and how I realized I was irritating myself over trivial matters, she asked, "What are you going to do, write a book about it?" We both began to laugh because we knew where the conversation would go next.

"What's the title of your book?" she asked.

I started to brainstorm book titles. *Why a Toddler Won't Sit Still after Drinking a Biggie Cup of Soda* or *How to Parent at 1:00 A.M. In the Airport* were just two working titles I shared. Eventually, my sister chimed in with additional suggestions. Ultimately, our list of titles became similar to other lists we created. Every time we generated book titles, one or more included an F-bomb followed by "LOL."

Dancing at my pity parties and Writing a Book About It were just two of many coping strategies I learned and started to practice. Since I began to feel some relief by using these and other tools, I wanted to share them along with a message about the need for mental health care for patients. Every time a doctor unintentionally gave me too much airtime, I got on my soapbox.

One such opportunity came during a discussion with my cardiologist. This conversation ended up being a catalyst for me to inventory all the tools I had accumulated thus far.

Sometime after my diagnoses, the results from my lung tests were stable, but I was again worried that my breathing had gotten worse. In addition to lung scarring, breathing can feel more labored in someone with scleroderma for many reasons including cold winter air, hot humid air, lack of muscle strength, and general stress. Heart problems can also cause breathing to become more difficult. Because of this, Dr. Lung recommended that I see my cardiologist, Dr. Heart.

Dr. Heart was a tall man with an athletic build. He wore round glasses before they were fashionable and sported a slightly smaller but just as noticeable Groucho Marx mustache. His voice was baritone deep and he was very personable. I trusted him immediately when I first met him years ago during the treatment for my thyroid issue. It was nice to see him again, although I wished the circumstances for our visit were different.

Dr. Heart asked a few questions and stated that the results of my recent echocardiogram suggested I needed a more invasive test to rule out excessive pressure in the blood vessel between my heart and lungs. Sweat formed under my arms and a knot grew in my throat. My old fears about developing pulmonary hypertension began drowning out the doctor's informative description of the right heart catheterization procedure. Eugene's voice appeared in my head: "You don't have a magic ball. You don't know the future." My attention toward Dr. Heart returned just in time for me to reach out and take the piece of paper he was handing me with information about the procedure (which, ultimately showed no extra pressure in my blood vessel.)

As my visit with Dr. Heart concluded, I sensed an opportunity to promote my mental health care message. "I've been seeing an excellent local therapist and have learned some tools to help me deal with the anxiety I've experienced since I was diagnosed," I said. "I ask myself questions when I start to generate negative thoughts."

"Is that so?" he said with real interest.

Leaning his back against the counter in the exam room, he then said, "Earlier this week, I met with a young woman I diagnosed with a severe heart condition. She's not handling the stress well. Would you be willing to share the questions you find helpful?"

His request was unexpected but also exciting. What an honor it would be to help someone else by sharing some of the tools I was using to calm myself! I was surprised, however, that after all the years Dr. Heart had been practicing, he didn't have resources available to help this woman. How was it possible that a cardiologist, who must tell several people each week that their life is hanging in the balance, did not even have a brochure on dealing with the emotional side of heart disease?

While I was surprised by this gap, research highlights the need for more attention to the mental health needs of patients, as well as the gap in medical training that would help physicians more effectively deal with these needs. For example, in the *American Journal of Geriatric Psychiatry*, Dr. Joseph Gallo, professor of mental health at Johns Hopkins University, writes that while "there's ample clinical and epidemiologic evidence that demonstrates that depression is higher among those who suffer from chronic illnesses, a gap exists in the medical care field where the emotional dimension of a patient is often overlooked. One of the reasons for this is that many physicians have not been trained to speak to patients about depression or behavioral health, in general" (2017, 520-521).

Dr. Heart's request provided me an opportunity to harvest all the tools, including the questions I had learned from my discussions with Eugene. Since many of the times I felt anxious were related to intrusive, scary thoughts, I knew one question I had to include in my imaginary mental health toolbox. It had become the first question I ask myself when I find myself starting to worry about a potential future event: Is it happening *now*?

Eugene had asked me this question several times, such as when I told him I was dying or that I couldn't breathe. The strategy of challenging my thoughts by asking what was happening now was helpful. I continued to create scary thoughts and images, like *My heart is failing*, or *My mucous is drowning me*, but asking myself, *Is it happening now?* often helped me break the continuous loop of the intrusive thought.

The reality of any given moment was often very different than what my thoughts were telling me. In general, I have found my thoughts to be lies. Sometimes, however, I couldn't tell if my thought was telling me something real, like when I thought, *Maybe my esophagus is really hardening?* or *Maybe my insurance really won't pay for this procedure?* Another question was needed in my toolbox: What action do I need to take? Perhaps I needed to dial 911, make an appointment with a doctor, or call my insurance company?

Ignoring or stuffing fears down was not my intent. Stuffing things down is a recipe for an explosion at some later date. If the fear is real, I should take action. If it is not real, then I must accept that I am generating thoughts and envision them flowing through and out of me.

My toolbox ended up taking the form of a written document which I titled *Calming the Worried Mind*. Despite Eugene's aversion to the word *mind*, I still used it. In the document, I identified three main activities: ask questions, redirect attention, and practice. Below are the items I placed in my toolbox:

Ask questions.

- Is my thought true? Is it true at this minute?
- Is the issue or concern out of my control?
- What action might I take if I remain concerned?

- What would I say to a loved one who had the same thought or concern?

Redirect attention.

- Go to my five senses (hearing, smell, touch, taste, and sight).
- Create a story that replaces the horror story I am currently telling; imagine writing a book about it.
- Turn my energy into art, poetry, or music.
- Schedule a Meeting to Worry.
- Take Action: make a call, go to the doctor, exercise, do an activity, or explore nature.
- Create a mantra to say each time I tell myself a lie.
- Talk to someone: a spouse, friend, therapist, or support group.
- Dance at my own pity parties.

Practice.

- Practice using the tools over and over again.

Apparently, I am not the only one who has created a list of helpful tools and techniques for dealing with anxiety and panic. Several months after making my own list of tools, I googled "tools for dealing with anxiety" and was surprised by the number of blog posts, magazine articles, and website pages on the topic. For a moment, I wondered why I had not searched for these resources at the beginning of my journey. Two reasons came to me: I was blinded by my fear of doing any research, and I felt overwhelmed by the darkness in my head.

Many of the suggested activities included in online resources are similar to what I've included in my own toolbox, but there are also many other suggestions for self-care, including:

- Focusing on your breathing
- Using guided imagery or visualization; downloading calming apps
- Meditating or praying
- Keeping a journal, writing, or creating gratitude lists

Health care providers might cringe at my suggestion that people go to the Internet to find tools for dealing with the worries they generate after being diagnosed with an illness, but if health care professionals were better trained on how to provide resources and care for the emotional side of illness or trauma, then patients and their families would not have to google information. Until then, patients and their caregivers should know there are resources available.

I sent Dr. Heart my document. He didn't let me know if he shared my ideas with his other patient, but I knew writing down the tools and questions for dealing with my moments of panic had been a useful exercise. It helped me recognized that I was becoming more resilient. Little did I know, however, that soon my ability to use these tools and strategies would be put to the test.

PART III

Accepting the Now: Bedtime Rituals

People create their own bedtime rituals to increase the chances that they will get at least a few hours of deep, uninterrupted sleep. Some read, some take melatonin, some drink a glass of wine, and some take a hot bath.

My bedtime routine starts with a cocktail.

Not a mojito, a cosmopolitan, or a Mai Tai—mine is a cocktail of medications. Before bed, I take a handful of pills, including a histamine two-blocker, an immunosuppressant, an anti-fibrotic, a synthetic thyroid hormone, and a cholesterol medicine.

Taking medicines is not the only way my bedtime ritual has changed since my diagnosis. Over time, the way I prepare for sleep has gotten more complex.

When I was in college, I could fall asleep anywhere. I fell asleep on a street bench while waiting for a ride in St. Croix and on a sofa in the basement of a building on the Johns Hopkins University campus. More than a few nights, I pulled an all-nighter because of my tendency to procrastinate on assignments. I had an occasional night when I dreamed about failing a test or going to class in my underwear. But, more times than not, the hours that I slept were deep and restorative.

By my mid-twenties, however, while in graduate school, I started having fitful nights. Since then, I rarely wake up feeling refreshed after a night of sleep. I learned to live with my sleep problems. Despite the change in quality of sleep, my bedtime routine remained relatively the same for years. I would strip down to a T-shirt and brush my teeth. That's it. I did not even wash my face, floss, or write in a gratitude journal.

When we had children, my husband and I set bedtime routines for them. Washing up, brushing teeth, putting on pajamas, spraying for monsters under the bed, and reading stories were evening activities. With two children we had to split the reading duties, but given my poor sleep from the previous night, I never remained awake throughout a whole children's book. Inevitably, I would wake to an elbow in my side and an angry plea, "Mommy, wake up. Finish the story!" Eventually, when the boys could read on their own or when we discovered books on tape, we let them lead their own bedtime activities.

Over time, my husband and I changed our own evening routine as well. Reading books or listening to the news in bed became common activities. Reading always made me fall asleep right away, but listening to the news had the opposite effect. My husband fell asleep with ease as all the world's problems were discussed on livestream news radio while I got increasingly upset. The news had the same effect on me as drinking a double espresso shot at 10:00 p.m. I suggested (or demanded, depending on who you ask) that we not listen to the news in bed.

Refreshing sleep is important for people with autoimmune diseases. Unfortunately, scleroderma, Raynaud's syndrome, acid reflux, lung disease, anxiety, and depression—as well as certain medicines—can impact sleep. This certainly is my experience.

As discomforts related to my diseases and medicines emerged over time, my ability to get a good night of sleep decreased. Pain, restless leg syndrome, stomach issues, coughing, nausea, dry eyes and mouth, and body temperature fluctuations became troublesome. To deal with these issues, I slowly made changes to my bedtime routine. After I dress for bed, brush my teeth, and take my cocktail of pills, I do the following: use eye drops and an oral rinse, lift the head of my bed with a wedge pillow, ensure a bottle of Tums is on the bedside table, navigate through the fifteen-to-thirty-minute wave of nausea that occurs after taking my medications, and turn on my bedside fan. Then, I deal with my feet.

Foot issues related to my Raynaud's syndrome are my biggest physical problem when trying to get a good night of sleep. I use to love musician Michael Frank's song "Popsicle Toes." Now, I see my own frozen toes as an incredible nuisance.

Even in the middle of the hot, North Carolina summer, my feet feel like blocks of ice as I crawl into bed. A hot shower or bath before bed can help resolve this problem, but on a typical night, I usually just put on warm socks and slip a hot water bottle between the sheets. Unfortunately, not long after warming up my feet, my soles begin to burn. They burn as if I am running barefoot on the Mojave Desert sands in the month of August. At this point, I kick off the socks and move aside the hot water bottle. I may also rub pain-killing gel or cream on my feet to take the edge off of the pain. Within a half hour, I will be able to ignore any lingering discomforts. At that point, I'm ready to sleep.

The good news is that I'm so tired after my time-consuming bedtime rituals, I fall right to sleep when I'm done.

CHAPTER 16.

Oxygen Drop

My legs stopped pushing, but my feet kept circling until the pedals on my stationary bike came to a stop on their own. Something didn't feel right.

In addition to my usual breathlessness, I felt drained and a little queasy. The reason for my sudden symptoms was not apparent. Maybe I was just tired? Or maybe it was too warm in the room? My goal had been to cycle with no resistance on the wheel for at least twenty minutes. After just seven minutes, I felt as if I was on the twenty-fifth mile of the Boston Marathon.

Given the circumstances, it made sense for me to check my oxygen level using my fingertip pulse-oximeter.

This device fits over the top of a fingertip and is small enough to be worn on a string around the neck if one needs to frequently measure their oxygen levels, as one might during periods of exercise. A couple of years ago, I purchased one because another pulmonary fibrosis patient I met through Dr. Lung talked about needing one to monitor themselves. It proved inexpensive and, like the medicines I started to hoard, having one made me feel like I had some control.

I slipped the oximeter on my index finger and waited for the reading. Within fifteen seconds, my reading appeared on the screen: eighty-four. A normal oxygen reading is 94 to 100 percent. I looked again: eighty-four.

Is this right? I questioned. *I think it's a bit low. Maybe it's deadly low?* My mind started to race about the significance of the value displayed on the oximeter. Continuing to exercise didn't seem safe, so I stopped.

My old stationary bike was off to the side in my home office, hidden from the camera on my computer that sat on my desk for zoom calls. Both pedals slightly drooped downward away from the bike, a characteristic that would be intolerable for any serious cyclist. A monitor was attached to the top of the handle bars to help me keep track of my miles, speed, distance, and calories burned. Stacks of important books and papers surrounded the bike on the floor, just far enough away as to not interfere with the bike pedals.

The plan was to create my own spin classes when I first purchased the bike on sale several years ago. After just a few rides, however, I realized that my purchase was an example of the old adage, "you get what you pay for." The narrow, uncomfortable seat and sagging pedals made riding the bike for any significant amount of time difficult. Fortunately for me, I was unable to ride for long. The quality of the bike matched my abilities perfectly now.

My motivation to exercise this day was the result of a commitment I had made to two friends. Earlier in the month, the three of us joined a virtual exercise challenge hosted by a local racing company. We signed up as a team under our old running group name, the Muffin Tops. Our team goal was to walk, run, cycle, or row a total of five hundred miles in three months from January to April 1, 2021. Spinning my legs, however slowly, was one way I could rack up some of the miles we needed.

Occasionally, I used the fingertip pulse oximeter, but they can be inaccurate for people with scleroderma and Raynaud's syndrome. These health problems can damage the blood vessels in the extremities, leading to false low readings or absent readings by the device. Despite this challenge, I reasoned that it would work on me if my hands were warm, an indication I had good blood flow to my fingers. When I didn't feel well on the bike, I decided to use the oximeter. I don't recall how warm or cold my hands were.

My oxygen levels during exercise had been monitored before. In early 2019, I enrolled in the pulmonary rehab program offered at the hospital. Each time I went to class the staff put an attractive and fashionable gray headband on me which held a sensor to my forehead. This sensor continuously monitored my pulse and oxygen levels. Everyone else in the class was monitored with the fingertip pulse oximeter. No matter what designer workout clothes I wore to the rehab class, my fashion look with the headband could only be described as "Hospital, 1970s."

Pulmonary rehab is a three-month exercise boot camp for people who can't breathe, including people with COPD, lung transplants, pulmonary fibrosis, or lung cancer. Similar to going to the gym, it also includes continuous monitoring of vital signs by nurses or other trained professionals. In rehab, I received an individualized exercise plan which included time on a stationary bike and treadmill.

The Tuesday-Thursday rehab exercise class included about fifteen people. Unfortunately, we didn't have much time for socializing, and since none of us could breathe well, chatting while on any of the machines was impossible. One day, however, we were asked to introduce ourselves at the start of the class. As we lined the back wall, an elderly gentleman wearing a faded yellow T-shirt and gray sweatpants stepped forward to begin.

"Hi, I'm John." He looked at the nurse as if to ask, *Should I say more?* Given her silence, he continued. "My doctor told me to come to this class because I have pulmonary fibrosis. I found out that people with PF have a life expectancy of three to five years. I was delighted to hear this because I'm eighty-two years old and I didn't think I had another three to five years."

A smile filled my heart and I thought, *I love that guy!* His impish grin after he introduced himself made me think he had some stories to tell. His humor was just what I needed that day. Unfortunately, I never saw him again.

Engaging in consistent exercise made me feel proud. I hadn't realized that prior to joining the class, I had been listening to the voice in my head that told me, *It's too dangerous to exercise.* But I did it; I finished the class. Much to the delight of my new rehab acquaintances, I wore my cap and gown from graduate school to do my final six-minute walk test around the rehab center. It was a graduation, after all. A week later, I climbed the hills in Lisbon, Portugal—slowly, but I still climbed them.

My exercise routine faltered upon my return from Portugal. The virtual exercise challenge I signed up for with my friends was an attempt to get back in the saddle, so to speak. When I saw the low oxygen readings, real or not, during my bike ride, I behaved in my usual modus operandi: I began catastrophizing. With the pulse oximeter still on my finger, my inner voice started its own repeating chorus. *You have just crossed the line. You now need oxygen to exercise. You have just crossed the line. You now need oxygen to exercise. You have just crossed the line. You now need oxygen to exercise.*

My body started to tingle as if I was being stabbed by a million little needles. Anxiety moved in like a black cloud before a North Carolina thunder storm. My heartbeat suddenly felt like a bass drum beating at the bottom of my throat. I could sense that I was headed for a panic attack. These were not new feelings. I recognized the gloom and doom rolling in like a tsunami. Despite the familiarity with the feelings, I was scared.

Many people with lung disease recognize the point of needing supplemental oxygen as a significant step in the progression of their disease. This is viewed as a red flag which tells you that your health is declining. If you were able to ignore your illness before, once you need oxygen, you can't. The need for oxygen complicates life tremendously. A person on oxygen must learn how to purchase oxygen, store oxygen, travel with oxygen, and regulate the flow of oxygen all without blowing up the house.

"Please. Please tell me this isn't true," I threw out into the universe.

Since the day I was diagnosed with lung disease, I created tests and milestones for myself. Each time I walked up the fifteen steps of the staircase to get to the second floor of my house, for instance, I quizzed myself. Was this walk faster or slower than the previous time I walked up the steps? Was I more out of breath or did I feel about the same as before? Often, needing an extra breath triggered me to think I needed oxygen.

All of the indicators of my disease getting worse were scary, but I was particularly afraid to reach the point of needing oxygen. This fear was one of the reasons I delayed connecting with the local pulmonary fibrosis support group after I was first diagnosed. Seeing people on oxygen, I told myself, was a peek into my future.

When I told Eugene this, he said, "I know you think you have the superpower of seeing into the future, but you don't. You don't know if you will need extra oxygen."

"If I need to go on oxygen, that will be it. My life will be over," I said dramatically.

"Over?" he questioned the absurdity of my statement. "Oxygen tanks are just a way to get oxygen. If you're at the point that you need to get extra oxygen, then you're just different. Our needs are always changing and we all must adapt as things change. The changes are not good or bad. They are just what is."

We sat in silence for a moment until Eugene added, "And, by the way, you're on oxygen now. We're all on oxygen."

His witty comment, as usual, broke the tension I felt. Eugene had made his point. If I needed to go on oxygen, that would be the card that life played and it would be neither good nor bad—to him maybe. To me, going on oxygen would be a terrible development.

After recording my oxygen levels that morning, I convinced myself that I was crossing the point of no return. The flood of anxiety I suddenly experienced blocked my access to all the lessons Eugene had taught me. All I could do was envision myself dragging a metal cylinder full of oxygen behind me, taking another step toward suffocation.

After about thirty minutes of rumination, I started to roam the house in search of an activity that would distract me. Unfortunately, the noise in my head left little energy for anything other than dealing with the worried thoughts. Ultimately, I curled up under a blanket in my favorite spot on the sofa. My mind kept going. Like a toddler trying to find the one pink sock somewhere at the bottom of the clothes hamper, I began mentally rummaging through my imaginary anxiety toolbox.

First, I asked myself, *Is it happening now? Do you need oxygen now?*

I don't know! I screamed in my head. I hadn't passed out, but maybe I was depriving my brain of the level of oxygen it needed.

Moving on, I decided to try recognizing what I was doing to myself. Between the reoccurring thoughts of doom, I forced myself to say aloud, "Donna, this is you. You are a worrier. Worrying is what you are doing right now." The intrusive thoughts didn't subside. Next, I reminded myself that I don't know what will happen. "Donna, you don't have a crystal ball. You don't know what the future looks like." Everything I said to myself felt like just words. I moved on.

Try a comedy show.

Read a book.

Nothing stopped the internal battle. I just couldn't relax or pay attention to anything but the jangling destructive thoughts in my head. Finally, after some period of time, it dawned on me to deploy my network of friends. I pulled out my phone and texted the women in one of my friend groups.

"It's about 1:20 p.m. Is anyone free right now for twenty minutes? I'm needing an ear so I can move a cloud from over my head. No worries if not." Immediately the phone rang and the texts started to pop up.

Jane wrote, "Sure, I'll call in a couple of minutes."
Laura wrote, "I'm on the phone with her now."
Kaci wrote, "Just seeing your note now. How about a conference call?"

A conversation with a trusted friend was my most powerful tool in my anxiety toolbox. Why had I waited so long to use it? Whatever the reason, it didn't make sense to kick myself.

When Laura called in response to my text, I felt relief. In my home office, I sat in the accent chair upholstered in faux brown leather made more for show than for prolonged use. The angle of the chair gave me a view of my backyard. At the time, however, I didn't notice how uncomfortable my chair was, nor did I notice the birds at the backyard bird feeder. You can't enjoy what is in front of you when you are in your head.

Laura and I spoke for at least an hour, during which I rattled off a fairly comprehensive list of catastrophes with hardly a breath between. For someone who said they couldn't breathe, I was clearly getting enough oxygen to rant. By the end of our conversation, I made the decision to take more action. Tomorrow, I vowed, I will call the doctor's office to make an appointment.

Fears over my potentially low oxygen levels were still with me, but the anguish I had been adding to my already heavy plate stopped.

A couple of weeks later when I saw Dr. Lung, my heart rate and oxygen levels were in normal range, but a few tests confirmed the decline in my breathing that I had noticed. When I was given this information, I accepted it. Maybe this was because I expected the results, or because I had already worked through my worry and grief.

Through this experience I recognized two things that will help me the next time I am struggling:

1. Keep trying different tools or actions when struggling; not every tool will work for every situation.
2. I'm thankful for my friends.

CHAPTER 17.

The Resilience Test: COVID-19

___

I need to say something, I thought as I overheard my son in the next room talking to his dad. *Say something. Say something!*

Being honest with my family suddenly felt like a matter of life and death. The situation necessitated that I share what I had kept to myself for the last four years.

In 2020, our lives took an unexpected turn. Both sons returned home because the COVID-19 pandemic altered their plans. Their activities, college classes at UNC-Chapel Hill, and an internship at Kennedy Space Center went online, and their summer job offers were withdrawn.

Our older son, who had dreams of working for NASA, took the new stay-at-home requirements as a challenge for any would-be astronaut. About a week or two after moving back home, I asked him, "Are you going stir-crazy being in your room all day, day after day?" Upbeat, he responded by saying, "If you can't spend long periods of time in a small, enclosed space, then you won't make it as an astronaut." Our younger son, on the other hand, viewed the time at home as an extended spring break. His high school friends had also returned home and all they wanted to do was visit with each other.

On this night, I was in my usual spot at one end of the wraparound sofa in our den. Dealing with my frozen feet and hands, I sat covered with my fleece electric throw blanket. Our home had an open floor plan. This allowed me to view the kitchen from the sofa with just a slight right turn of my head. As I sat scrolling through my phone, I overheard my youngest son pick his car keys up off the kitchen counter and tell my husband he was going to hang out with his friends. Being away at college had apparently given him the impression he could come and go as he pleased while in our house. In a normal situation, we may have given him that freedom as long as he respected the boundaries we set for our home. But the times were not normal. We were in the midst of a worldwide pandemic.

No one needed to tell me about the potential dangers of the virus, COVID-19. I had worked in public health for over twenty-five years and had studied crisis preparedness for my doctoral dissertation. I was aware of the ways in which infectious diseases spread as well as the history of other deadly pandemics, like the 1918 Spanish flu (1918–1919) the HIV/AIDS pandemic (1981–present), the Swine flu (2009–2010), and the Ebola outbreak (2014–2016). At this time, however, I viewed this situation with an additional lens, as a person with significant lung disease and a compromised immune system.

Given my health status, I started paying attention to the spread of COVID-19 before most Americans. In February 2020, I reached out to Dr. Lung to ask what advice he was giving to his pulmonary fibrosis patients regarding the threat. Through my online medical record, his office sent me this note.

Ms. Dinkin,

Dr. Lung stated that you should continue your regular medications daily, especially the OFEV. He also stated that you could stop the immunosuppressant drug for two months to reduce the immune suppression that it causes, but just know that there is a risk of the pulmonary fibrosis getting worse. Dr. Lung also wants you to practice extreme social distancing for eight to ten weeks, keep your hands washed, and use hand sanitizer.

My husband and I were well-practiced at hibernating by the time the rest of the world started to shut down. Fortunately, we were both comfortable with being home. Home was my husband's favorite vacation location. More so than many, he welcomed the changes in social expectations brought on by the pandemic. Working from a home office for over twenty years, I was also comfortable interacting with people over the phone or by computer instead of in person. We knew that if we needed to continue to hunker down for the next eight to ten weeks, we could handle it.

By mid-March 2020, the steady barrage of reports on the shortages of ventilators, personal protective equipment, and rising mortality rates, especially in the elderly and those with chronic conditions, had me troubled and frightened. I began experiencing terrifying nightmares which included vivid images of myself unconscious, or worse yet, conscious, on a ventilator machine, and all alone. Rhythmic hissing—*whoosh-silence, whoosh-silence*—filled the hospital room as the machine cycled.

Each morning, I woke exhausted. As the day went on, however, I energized myself with rage-filled conversations in my head or with my husband about pandemic news or about the people not following public health recommendations.

Unapologetic in my judgment of others, I found myself talking to my computer screen and TV as I looked at pictures on Facebook of friends gathering with others and as the news showed politicians not modeling preventive measures. The cars driving down the street in my neighborhood also triggered additional insufferable rants.

"Look, honey. Come here." I urged my husband to join me at the bay window in the front of our house to watch neighbors driving down our street, toward the road that connected our neighborhood to the rest of the world.

"Where are these people going? Don't they know that we are in a *pandemic*?" I angrily said as if I ruled the world.

Of course, I knew it was none of my business. The intellectual part of my brain knew some people needed a walk in the park to clear their heads and some with jobs in healthcare were on their way to save lives. Despite my internal reasoning, I kept generating the thoughts, *They are going to kill me and they don't care.*

My husband had a remarkable ability to watch the day's news without experiencing any rise in blood pressure. When our boys were small, he would tell them, "Put your shields up," a *Star Trek* reference, as a reminder to let the frustrations of the world not get to them. I tried to be Teflon, but at the time, I felt more like a magnet for frustration, judgment, and worry. I was struggling.

Eugene's voice played in my head. *It seems you want to make yourself mad. What are you getting from making yourself mad?*

It's easier to be mad than to deal with my fears of getting sick and being on a ventilator, I answered, deciding not to start an imaginary fight with Eugene over the assertion that I *wanted* to be mad.

On the night that my son reached for the car keys so he could go see friends, I began to panic. As long as the people in our home stayed in the house or in our yard, I felt safe. However, my heart started to race and my head became flooded with an infinite loop of frantic thoughts if any of us interacted with other people. I wondered how I could get my son to change his plans without ordering him to stay home. Before I said anything, I heard my husband speak up.

"The CDC is recommending that people not socialize. This will be over soon and then you can visit with your friends," he said logically.

As only a college student would say, our son responded, "I'll be safe. I'm an adult now. I can make my own decisions."

You're in our house. You need to follow the house rules! I yelled in my head.

In spite of the fact that I had been experiencing uncontrollable rage and anxiety, I still had the wherewithal to know that starting an argument with my son would not get me the results I wanted. But as I sat, knees to my chest in my spot on the sofa, I began to question myself. *Maybe I'm being too dramatic? Maybe I am being overly cautious? Maybe I'm a bad mother or a helicopter mother? No. No, no, no. It doesn't matter. He can't go out.*

At that point, I decided not to lecture him on the public health reasons for staying close to home but to share why *I* needed him to stay home. To do this, I needed to be more transparent about what I had been dealing with—the part I wanted to keep locked up.

I did not share the full impact of my diseases with those closest to me. My family members—including my husband, my children, my siblings, and my parents, when they were alive—knew I had been diagnosed with something that affected my lungs, but I looked fine and, for the most part, I acted fine. They also knew I was working with Eugene, but when I shared aspects of my therapy experience, I kept the description superficial. The deep emotional suffering I was experiencing was locked in a box in my head. Unconsciously, I decided to fly a good part of this experience solo as I had with other aspects of my life, like travel and work.

Why didn't I share my whole experience with others? Why haven't I had many people join me at doctor appointments? And why haven't I let others fully into my room of darkness and despair? Partly, I made these choices because I wanted to protect the people I love from worrying. This was true particularly when it came to my children. I did not want my sons' childhoods to be burdened with the experience of a sick, depressed mother. The whole truth, however, is really more self-serving.

First, I shut people out because I didn't think I could handle their reactions or their worries about my health or prognosis. For example, one day my mother and I were talking on the phone as I drove to an appointment at Duke Medical Center.

"Please don't tell me you're suffering! I couldn't handle that," she said in response to my factual statement about the day's appointment.

Trying to end that line of questioning, I quickly said, "No, of course not. I'm fine. Don't worry." I did not want to take care of the emotions of others while I was struggling to take care of my own emotions.

Second, I didn't think I could handle people's generosity and consideration, such as when friends insisted on meeting my needs over their own needs or those of a group. This had happened when a group of friends rescheduled a dinner reservation to 5:30 p.m. instead of the usual 7:30 p.m. to accommodate the management of my reflux issues, which occurred if I ate too late. Despite the wonderful feeling of being cared for, I struggled accepting both the love and the spotlight on my weird set of needs.

Finally, I couldn't handle my own expectations that I be pleasant and present with others if they had joined me at a doctor visit. My husband and a few friends have accompanied me to various appointments or medical tests over the years. Sometimes it has been necessary to have a functioning adult drive me home after a medical procedure. Other times, loved ones have wanted to show support during a potentially stressful time. I appreciated their support and generosity. However, I found it difficult to be conversational or "normal" when I just wanted to be in my own head.

On the night my son told us he was going out to visit friends, he was unaware of my emotional state over the COVID-19 pandemic and how my reaction was linked to my fears about my health. As my son walked to the door, keys in hand, I yelled across the den into the kitchen, "Can I speak to you for a minute?" I remained huddled under my blanket, thinking any movement may cause me to explode into a million pieces.

He walked into the den begrudgingly and said, "Mom, I know what you're going to say."

"No, you don't." I looked at him while I moved one hand to my chest to keep my beating heart from bursting through my skin. Something inside tried to stop me from speaking, but something else urged me on. "I need to tell you that I've been hiding something from you." I paused to catch my breath. Fear always tightened my chest and made it harder to breathe.

"I've not shared with you how scared I have been over my health issues and how my fear has grown since the pandemic started." Batting my eyelids to contain the tears welling up, I continued, "I believe it would be very unsafe for me to get coronavirus. It's important for you to know how frightened I feel." I didn't say anything else. Mentally, I started rebuilding the wall I had just taken down.

My son grunted, "Um, okay," and then slowly walked back in the kitchen. "I'm going for a drive." Car keys in hand, he walked out of the house.

Frozen in place, I wondered why I had been unable to manage my emotions, particularly after all the counseling I had received. My coping strategies to deal with anxiety were ineffective. Now, I believed, I'd also traumatized my son by telling him the truth about my frailties.

My son came home for the summer at the time of this writing. It seemed like a good time to apologize for scaring and upsetting him with my health concerns that evening in 2020. In response to my apology, he said, "I wasn't upset. I just needed to get out because I felt cooped up." Clearly, I still thought I had the superpower of knowing what other people were thinking.

CHAPTER 18.

Art and the Roseate Spoonbill

In the early months of the pandemic, I created a tornado of negativity. Because of my inability to manage my emotions, particularly after all the work I had done with Eugene, I was disappointed in myself. I thought my anxiety toolkit was missing a key tool that could help me control my rogue thoughts. It took me the whole year, but a piece of chalk, a boat, and a bird showed me I was wrong.

My original goal in seeking mental health counseling was to learn how to stop the panic and anxiety I experienced after my initial diagnoses in 2015. As I talked with Eugene, I realized the path for someone with a chronic or progressive disease is more like a roller coaster ride than a walk on a boardwalk. I experienced a lot of ups and downs in my journey and I needed to be able to deal with them. At that point, I decided to expand my personal therapy goals to include "become more resilient."

I didn't think becoming more resilient or better at adapting or bouncing back would mean I would never face another challenge or I would never have fears or other negative thoughts. Eugene had made it quite clear to me that I would never stop worrying and I just needed to accept the fact that I was a worrier. Scleroderma had also made it clear that I would face some good and some challenging physical health days. Even if you don't have scleroderma or some other health condition, if you have been lucky enough to age, you're on a similar roller coaster ride. Those of us who can build resiliency will add less suffering to our days. That's what I intended to do, but I told myself the tools I had been using to calm my worried mind were not working when I found myself struggling again.

When I wasn't paralyzed by my own fear and rage in 2020, I filled my time with various activities. We grilled dinner outside with the boys, went on walks in the neighborhood, watched the news on TV, cooked new recipes, engaged with friends on Zoom, and searched Netflix for the next great drama series. By summer, when the world started to open back up, my husband and I decided to remain physically isolated from other people. In my mind, the only way I would remain free from exposure to coronavirus was to protect myself. My husband, thankfully, was fully supportive of us maintaining distance from others.

One day as I roamed from room to room in our home, a new favorite activity, I spotted a pad of paper and a pastel art kit I had purchased years ago. These items were placed on a shelf with the thought that one day I would have the time and energy to enjoy them. My desire to create art was not completely out of the blue. My mother and grandmother enjoyed painting, and as a teen, I sketched pictures copied from magazines lying around the hair salon my dad owned. My sons were also both artists. My oldest had even been enrolled in a visual arts program for high school. I collected pencils and paper over the years but never really sat long enough to let the creative spirit take over. For some reason, perhaps because the world had stopped and I had to find ways to fill my time, I suddenly felt interested.

Gathering the supplies off of the shelf, I went to the kitchen where there was plenty of light and a sizable table to work. I moved the salt and pepper shakers from the middle of the table and spread out my paper and sticks of twenty assorted colors of chalk. When I couldn't decide what to draw, I pulled out my iPhone and searched the Internet for a simple piece of art to copy. The self-doubt that once stifled my creativity no longer had space in my head. If Picasso could become famous for his distorted art images, I could do it too. After googling terms like "colorful art" and "famous artists," I found a colorful cubist image by Brazilian artist Romero Britto of the late artist Frida Kahlo. This served as the inspiration for my first piece of COVID-period art.

I pulled myself closer to the table. My notebook, opened to a blank page, begged for some color. With a No. 2 pencil in hand, I sketched a simple outline of Frida's face and flowered headpiece. To represent a bulky, beaded necklace, I drew a string of circles around the base of her neck. I took my black chalk stick and marked lines through my outline, making the drawing look like a stain glass window. Then, I colored. I colored like a child with a coloring book. Red, blue, yellow, green, and black chalk dust covered the table top, my hands, and my clothing. In the end, I had a vibrant, Picasso-esque Frida Kahlo portrait.

Each morning, I found myself back at the table. The rising sun shined into my kitchen through the windowed doors that opened to the back deck. The house was quiet. My boys were back in their college towns and my husband relaxed in another room with AirPods in his ears, listening to various podcasts or the news. I sat in my new favorite spot and placed my coffee cup far enough from my creative space to not ruin my art in the event of a spill. I drew. Some pieces were landscapes, some were portraits, some were still life, and some were just abstract blobs of color and lines. During this time my head was quiet. I heard no intrusive thoughts, no worries, and no chatter. *Is this what Zen feels like?* I wondered.

Over a six-month period, I drew about ninety-four-by-six-inch art pieces. Most of the pastel drawings were miniature copies of pieces created by other talented artists, such as Jean-Michel Basquiat, Amedeo Modigliani, Trisha Adams, Victor Ekpuk, and Cathleen Rehfeld. My favorite inspirations, however, came from portrait artist Nancy Rosen and landscape artist Peter Batchelder. Nancy is well known for the placement of her art in the Netflix series *Grace and Frankie*. I love the rich expressions of weariness of the women in her portraits. Peter Batchelder's simple scenes of barns and small cottages took me back to my New England roots. Both artists include wonderful colors in their creations.

I was amazed at the calming effect making art had on me. As autumn arrived, I noticed I was enjoying not only the colors of the pastel chalks, but also the changing hues of the maple tree leaves outside my kitchen windows. Soon, I found myself wanting to get outside and enjoy nature.

For my sixtieth birthday in late 2020, I requested an outdoor adventure. An exotic trip or a big birthday bash were not options due to the pandemic, so instead, I asked my husband to go kayaking with me in our neighborhood pond. We had purchased two fiberglass kayaks years ago for my son who once had shown an interest in kayaking. Once or twice over the years, we floated around the pond, but mostly they laid untouched under our back deck.

Our local pond is at the end of our street, just one hundred feet past the small neighborhood pool and unevenly paved tennis court. Some neighbors who live along one side of the pond, occasionally launch fishing boats into the water from their own docks, but for the most part, the entire pond is human free. A blue heron has claimed the pond as his own, and if one is patient, they can see that the pond is home to numerous species of other birds and wildlife. After thirty years of living in the neighborhood, I was shocked to realize we had almost entirely ignored this gem of tranquility right in our own backyard.

The pond in no way compares to the majesty of Lake Winnipesaukee, NH, where my dad owned a cottage and we went each summer as young adults. The pond is muddy, shallow, and small. The water in Lake Winnipesaukee is expansive, cold, deep, and clear. Despite their differences, when I paddled my kayak in the muddy pond, I felt the same breeze, I heard the same ripple of water, and I saw the same turtles diving off of their logs into the water. All of my senses were in use as I floated. While paddling, I was incapable of creating any horror stories about the future. My only thoughts were, *Where is my heron friend?* and *How am I going to lift myself out of this kayak?* (Okay, so I did create one negative thought.)

The mental health benefit of being out in nature should not have surprised me. I had once heard that getting out in nature was part of the national public health strategy in Japan. As reported by *National Geographic*, forest bathing, absorbing the forest atmosphere, emerged as a Japanese practice in the 1980s. The purpose was to serve as an eco-treatment to tech-boom burnout but also to gain support for protecting the country's forests (Fitzgerald 2019). Science supported what I was also beginning to learn for myself: spending time in nature was good for the head, heart, and soul.

During the summer of 2021, I noticed a headline from the local newspaper: "Rare Spoonbill Sighting at Oak Hollow Lake Excites Local Birders" (Tomlin 2021). It seemed a roseate spoonbill had been sighted at the lake. This sighting was newsworthy because the pink, flamingo-like bird with a long spoon-shaped bill was rarely seen this far north or this far inland, approximately two hundred miles from the ocean. Local birdwatchers flocked to the lake to see if they could add a sighting to their Life List—a list of birds seen in a lifetime. While I wasn't a birder, a birdwatcher who actively seeks to find different species of birds, I had always been interested in seeing them.

I learned about birders in my forties when I pulled the book *To See Every Bird on Earth* by Dan Koeppel (2006) off the

"Dirt Cheap" bookshelf at a local bookstore. Koeppel writes about his father's lifetime obsession of finding birds after spotting a brown thrasher at age twelve. The bird that transformed my regard for nature into an above-average interest in birds turned out to be the roseate spoonbill. I had to see it.

Two weeks after I read the news article, the spoonbill was no longer seen at the lake mentioned in the story and I believed I had missed my chance to see it. However, I soon learned that local birders had started seeing a pair of roseate spoonbills at another local lake. My son was home and willing to go with me on a bird hunt. We had to walk on trails to get to the part of the lake where the birds were being spotted.

After my lung disease diagnosis, I convinced myself I could no longer hike in the woods because of my breathing challenges. My determination to find this pair of birds, however, overshadowed the fears I had created about walking on trails. I reasoned that if my son was with me, I would have the courage to try walking the hilly trail that led to the lake. He agreed and we set off one afternoon with binoculars in hand to Palmetto Trail, a trail that followed the edge of Lake Brandt in Greensboro, NC.

We parked the car at the entry to the trail and began walking. The dirt trail was about six feet wide and lined by trees and thick undergrowth on both sides. My son and I had the forest to ourselves. A thought entered my head as we started. *Am I setting the stage for my son to have to rescue me from a breathing event, thereby causing him additional trauma to what I caused that night in 2020?* (This, I now know, was a story I told myself, and it ended up not being true. Apparently, he was not traumatized.) I quickly acknowledged the thought was not a current reality. I stopped walking, leaned slightly back, and visualized the thought flowing through me like a leaf floating along a rushing stream. It was gone.

The trail was relatively flat, much to my surprise. We heard birds singing around us. We saw squirrels rummaging in the bushes or jumping from tree to tree. The trail meandered around the edges of the lake's southeast edge. We slowly climbed a small hill, probably not noticeable to most people, about three-tenths of a mile into our hike. I noticed that my breathing had become labored, so I suggested we stop. From our location, we could get a partial view of an area of the lake called the mudflats. Local birders have recorded over two hundred species of birds in this area, and this was where the roseate spoonbills had been most recently sighted. Maybe we did not need to go any further? While I caught my breath, we scanned the area with our eyes. Soon, I noticed two pinkish dots on the other side of the lake. With the binoculars, it became clear that we had found our lovebird pair.

"Oh my," I first mumbled as I focused the binocular lenses. I followed this with a squeal loud enough to disturb other wildlife in the area. "We found them!"

My son, who had much more control over his emotions, reached his hand out for the binoculars. "Let me see," he demanded. Leaning over the brush surrounding us, he adjusted the lenses to find the birds. Once he saw them, he calmly said, "Cool." I followed his comment with a happy dance that would belie the health of my lungs and challenge any dance I had taken at one of my pity parties. You would have thought I was seeing a natural wonder like the Grand Canyon, Mount Everest, or Victoria Falls. The joy I felt at that moment was more than one would have expected for the situation. I was happy not only because I saw some rare birds, but also because I smashed the story I had been telling myself: that I couldn't hike. It felt like a big moment.

Before I knew it, I was visiting area lakes, fields, and trails on a regular basis. On my phone, I downloaded an app that provided the level of difficulty for various trails and a birding app that could identify bird songs around me at any given time. I began to realize that it was impossible to listen for birds and worry at the same time. Instead, I was practicing curiosity and using my senses. I was paying attention to the moment in front of me.

One day, as I sipped my morning coffee and contemplated my day's activities, I realized my step had felt lighter, my smile wider, and my attitude better—not perfect, but better! Why did I feel better mentally when my physical health was continuing to slowly decline? Why did I feel better when the world continued to be in chaos?

After reflecting for a few minutes, I realized I had been moving toward the things I wanted to spend more time doing, as identified in my visualization project. With those activities, I had been practicing the tools from my imaginary anxiety toolbox. It took me a while to learn how to apply my tools to a different type of personal crisis—illness versus the world falling apart—but they worked.

In the spring of 2022, about six months after my bird-watching obsession started, I went for a walk in a park with a good friend. We regularly went for walks and she had heard my stories about being diagnosed, entering the clinical drug trial, not having diarrhea and then having it, being scared about COVID-19, and being angry at the world. She knew about my work with Eugene and had also decided to see him not long after I started my visits back in 2015. We often processed our therapy sessions together, which led to greater insights for me. On this particular walk, I told her about the joy I was experiencing from my art and nature excursions.

"Eugene would be happy to hear how far I've come—how far we've both come!" I said as we stopped on a bridge to scan the lake for herons.

"Actually," my friend pointed out, "he would say, 'You don't know how I feel.'" We laughed.

Neither of us had seen Eugene since the beginning of 2020. We were both affected by a change in health insurance. Our insurance no longer covered visits with him.

"It's disgusting that insurance can dictate who you see for your mental health care," I blurted out with frustration.

She agreed and responded, "It is not easy to change therapists after working with one for a while. And we both know there's no one like Eugene!"

The possibility of continuing to see Eugene by paying out of pocket for the sessions crossed my mind, but ultimately I decided I had the tools needed to deal with my health and aging journeys. At that point, it was just a matter of practicing. When COVID-19 hit just a couple months later, Eugene also started to consider retirement. He was eighty years old, and while he was in great health, the social distancing requirements from the pandemic response were impacting the practice of psychotherapy.

I first went to Eugene when I was in crisis. Actually, if crisis is both danger and opportunity—as I had tattooed on my hip all those years ago—I was only in the danger part. After working with Eugene and practicing what I learned through the ups and downs of my diseases, the pandemic, and life in general, I moved into the opportunity part. Danger still lurks, but the opportunity to learn about myself has been one of the great benefits coming from my crisis.

When I think of the lessons I pulled from Eugene's quips and sage advice, I see they fall into three categories: acceptance, curiosity, and connection. I am practicing acceptance. Shit happens, I am who I am, and others are who they are. I am practicing curiosity. The moment in front of me is fascinating, the person in front of me is fascinating, and Greensboro is fascinating. I am practicing connection. Friends and family help even the solo traveler get through the journey.

On that spring day as my friend and I continued to walk, she pointed to a pair of birds sitting on a phone line stretched between poles at the park. With their faint blue color and brown spotted chests, identifying what kind of birds they were was difficult from a distance. As we got a little closer, I said, "Those are juvenile eastern bluebirds."

Some people believe that bluebirds symbolize happiness and fulfillment. The meanings attributed to these beautiful birds also describe where my mind is right now—happily fulfilled.

CHAPTER 19.

Next Thursday

I called Eugene the other day.

We've talked on the phone a few times since I last saw him in January 2020. I always feel a bit awkward when I call, not knowing if I am still a patient or a friend. *Why does it matter?* I question myself. *I know that I care about him. That's all that matters.*

The first time I called, I wanted to ask if he was still seeing patients. I knew someone looking for some support. I also wanted to see how he was doing since he lived alone and the pandemic was isolating people. He assured me he was fine and that while he enjoyed being with people, he was also an introvert. I knew he didn't judge what was happening before him, so if a pandemic was keeping him in the house for a while, it was neither good nor bad.

During one of our calls a few months back, I told him about my effort to process our time together, confirming that I was practicing what I had learned. I was reflecting by reading the journal I had written in each time we met, but also by penning my story in the form of a memoir. He was delighted to hear of my activities and said I could share his real name and any of the stories he had shared with me in my writings. I limit what I share, but anything I do share about him is true or is how I interpreted his story. I kept a fictitious name, but I've had several friends asked if Eugene is the unconventional and brutally honest therapist many of us know. Yes, he is.

During our call the other day, Eugene mentioned that he's in good health and is enjoying time working out at the gym, doing yoga, and going cycling. While he officially retired from his group practice, he sees some clients and still does some teaching on Gestalt therapy via Zoom. He is booked to go on a trip to Argentina and Antarctica this coming winter.

My physical health continues to slowly decline, as determined by my pulmonary function test results, but I continue to get my oxygen the old fashion way, from the air. I take my time getting up staircases and make a scene when I try to lift myself out of my kayak, but I still do these things. Dr. Lung and Dr. SSc connected recently to talk about my current treatment plan. They decided and I agreed to stay the course on all of my medicines. In reality, there aren't many options to try. After five and half years, the OFEV clinical drug trial I participated in will end in three months. I anticipate that I will need tools from my imaginary toolbox to help me get through the stress I will generate while seeking ways to pay the $12,000-per-month drug cost. Right now, I'm deciding to not write that "murder mystery." I'll cross that bridge when I get to it.

I continue to work on small projects related to leadership development and evaluation. I'm thankful I can pick the projects that are meaningful to me and that I can do from the comfort of my sofa—I mean, my office. I enjoy the company of my friends on walks, at book club meetings, and at an occasional dinner at a restaurant, all outdoors. I'm not exercising and I have decided to ignore Eugene's voice in my head, which says, I must not want to exercise, because I'm not doing it (he's right, of course).

On my desk, I still have a ticket for a flight to Australia and New Zealand which was originally booked for February 2020. For now, however, I'm enjoying art, roseate spoonbills, and whatever else is in front of me in Greensboro, NC.

At the end of our call, I suggested to Eugene that we meet for coffee or tea. He countered with a much better alternative. How about we meet for ice cream?

We made a date.

Acknowledgments

I've avoided writing my entire life, but I knew I had a story to tell. My hope is that by telling it I can support others going through a difficult time. If not, I know the process of writing my story down at least helped me. I am extremely grateful to a number of people who helped me turn my story into a book.

I want to thank my family members. My husband, Sylvester Taylor, and our sons, Joseph and Noah, encouraged me to write a book even though they had no idea what I would say about them or what it would cost us. They have loved me through the writing process but also through so much more. I also want to thank my sister, Cheryl Dinkin, her husband, Dan Graham, my brother, David Dinkin Flynn, and my second mother, Donna Gaudette, for their support and willingness to rehash old family stories. I'm particularly grateful for all the times over the course of our lives they made me laugh so hard I cried. I never realized until writing this book how important that level of laughter is to me.

I'm grateful to my closest girlfriends, who have supported me throughout life but also during the long journey to become mentally well after my diagnoses. I have many friends to thank but I want to lift those who remained close and didn't run away after I *repeatedly* shared my worries, the details of each medical test, and my stories of medicine side effects. Thank you, Tracy Patterson, Ann Morris, Susan Kroll-Smith, Sara King, Katherine Weaver, and Brenda Motsinger McAdams. To all my friends who have supported me, my sky is much brighter because of you.

I'd like to thank my three main doctors, Dr. Lung, Dr. Rheumatology, and Dr. Scleroderma (Dr. SSc). Early on each of them asked what I was concerned about, and when I said, "I just want to see my children grow up," they knew that I meant, "I just want to see my children grow up to age fifty." That's what they've been helping me do. Thanks for always seeing me as a person first.

I want to share a special thank you to all of the people who helped me improve my storytelling abilities. My friends who volunteered to be beta readers (*) read a few sections of my book. The suggestions and cheerleading messages they sent helped me continue to move forward. My three Super Readers—Ann Morris, Steve Kroll-Smith, and Lisa Napoli, editor extraordinaire—who read the whole second draft, warts and all, jumped in despite a ridiculously short timeline and weren't afraid to give me the honest feedback I needed. It was a gift. My development editor, Trisha Giramma, and my revisions editor, Megan Hart, who read my chapters over and over and over again—I owe you a great debt for helping me to see both the big picture and the minute details of my story. You continued to champion my effort even when I struggled with self-confidence. Had I known the importance of having a village to write prior to this project, I would have called each of you when I was writing my doctoral dissertation. You got me through this process much quicker and with a lot less pain than the dissertation.

Thanks to all of my friends, family members, school classmates, and colleagues who believed in me and in my book without knowing or seeing any evidence that I was actually sitting down at my computer to write. The love you showed me during my pre-sale campaign was overwhelming. During this outpouring of support, I realized a lot of people were going to read my book. That scared me to death, but it also put the fire under me. I still feel the warmth of your love to this day.

Roxann Tomao Burney*
Donna L. Gaudette
Susan Goldstein*
Vonna Henry*
Ellen Wolf*
Melodie Howard
Jo-Ann Lopiccolo
Amy Z. Rose
Joseph S. Taylor
Richard Dinkin
Ann Morris
Lucinda Lynn Earle*
Noah D. Taylor
Cheryl Dinkin*
Meg Molloy*
Carolyn Satoh*
Brenda Willis

Linda Gallagher
Christina Soyun Park
Valerie Bateman
Corinne Hamilton
Debbie Clark
Tracy Patterson*
Elliot Axelrod
Pam Larson
Kristi Slomski
Brenda McAdams*
Anna Schenck
Ron Gordon*
Souad Benelhamdia
Alicia Archibald
Sylvia Coleman
Bethann Gibbs*
Lily Kelly Radford*
Magda Peck*
Kathy Ferretti
Jennifer Martineau
Joyce Gaufin*
Heather Champion
Lynn Fick-Cooper
Martha Shafer
David Dinkin Flynn
Diane Weber
Karin Wiedemann
Karen Mill*
Katherine Weaver*
Barbara Demarest
Sandy Riha
Lisa Stahlmann Jessar

Whitney Davis
Unsil Ko Kiser
Nathan Denkin*
Nancy Tolliver
Cheryll Lesneski
Ellen Gefen
Jennifer Davis
Jean Wolf*
Sara King
Charlotte Matheny
Shirley Landry
Brooke Monaghan
Karen Hills
Trisha Giramma
Cynthia Lamberth
Christina Brown
Kelly Hannum
Kate Panzer
Sunjin Harrington
Corinne Ehrlich
Debbie Lieberman
Eric Koester
Rhea Egbert
Martha Hughes-James
Susan Kroll-Smith*
Rosemary Ireland
Laura Mauceri
Shannon Allen
Nancy Probst
Wendy Mccain
Kris Novelli
Suzanne Hawley

Cathy Slemp
Debbie Reisner
Jennifer Weathersby
Dan Graham
Steve Kroll-Smith
Rosanna Tufts*
Susan Parris Ray*
Michelle Schneider
Dawn Barts
Nance Smithwick
Andi Williams
Beth King*
Steve Frederick
Deb Geiss
Ellen Van Velsor
Hilary V. Greene
Emma Meiden
Lisa Bearden
Julie Best Chase*
James Davis
Heather Mchugh
Ken Gordon
Margaret Grun Kibben
Ellen Loring
Peter Swartz
Mary Malcolmson
Sarah Glover
Lyndon Rego
Stephen Jennings
Winn Legerton
Pia Macdonald
Alicia Kay*

Thayle & David Heggie
Ann Houston Staples
Racquel Graham
Stephanie Bartis
Junean Lanigan
Julie Ann Cooper
Mark Holt
Jennie Mullins
Stephen J. Luber
Isabel Geller*
Sylvester Taylor
Felix Jahncke
Rhonda Markowitz
Stan Gryskiewicz
Deborah Slazyk
Lissa Eaton*
Marie Flake
Shelley Reynolds
Robert Earl*
Rachel Peterson
Robert Elliott
Kathy Fitch
Ruth Heyd
Fran Atchison
Heather Braddy

Special thanks to the extraordinary artist, my son Joseph Taylor, who made the roseate spoonbill art pieces and notecards that were part of my campaign. His talent is amazing, but his offer to help and support me in this journey is what makes me so proud to be his mom.

Finally, I'd like to thank Eugene, the person with the greatest impact on my story. I apologize to him for all of the off-limit words I used while writing this book, but I take ownership for using them. I am tremendously grateful that he has been by my side for this part of my journey. Thank you.

Appendix

Author's Note
Riggs, Nina. 2017. *The Bright Hour.* New York: Simon & Schuster, Inc.

1. The Diagnosis
Saget, Bob. 1996. *For Hope.* Columbia TriStar Television. 1 hour 40 minutes.

3. I Can't Handle the Truth
Yasuoka, H. 2015. "Recent Treatments of Interstitial Lung Disease with Systemic Sclerosis." *Clinical Medicine Insights: Circulatory, Respiratory and Pulmonary Medicine* 9s1, (December): 97–110. https://doi.org/10.4137/CCRPM.S23315.

4. Catastrophizing

Mayo Clinic Staff. April 13, 2022. "Pulmonary hypertension." Mayo Clinic. Accessed October 27, 2022. https://www.mayoclinic.org/diseases-conditions/pulmonary-hypertension/symptoms-causes/syc-20350697.

5. The Me Before

Chen, Lincoln C., and Kevin S. Scrimshaw, eds. 1983. *Diarrhea and Malnutrition: Interactions, Mechanisms and Interventions,* New York, NY: Springer Publisher.

7. How are you?

Harvey, Paul. 2022. *Paul Harvey Radio Shows.* Read by Paul Harvey. Oakville, ON, Hexagon Tech. Audible audio ed., 15 hr., 40 min.

8. Am I In The Fight?

Kubrick, Stanley. 1980. *The Shining.* Warner Bros. 2 hours 24 minutes.

9. Controlling the Uncontrollable

Distler, Oliver, Kristin B. Highland, Martina Gahlemann, Arata Azuma, Aryeh Fischer, Maureen D. Mayes, Ganesh Raghu, et al. 2019. "Nintedanib for Systemic Sclerosis—Associated Interstitial Lung Disease." *New England Journal of Medicine* 380, (June): 2518–2528. https://www.nejm.org/doi/10.1056/NEJMoa1903076.

13. Ben & Jerry's
Jonasson, Jonas. 2012. *The 100-Year-Old Man Who Climbed Out the Window and Disappeared*. New York: Hachette Books.

14. Time Well Spent
Kalanithi, Paul. 2016. *When Breath Becomes Air*. London: Penguin Random House.

Lamott, Anne. 1994. *Bird by Bird*. New York: DoubleDay.

15. The Imaginary Toolbox
Gallo, Joseph J. 2017. "Multi-Morbidity and Mental Health." *The American Journal of Geriatric Psychiatry* 25, no. 5 (May): 520–521. https://doi.org/10.1016/j.jagp.2017.02.007.

18. Art and the Roseate Spoonbill
Fitzgerald, Sunny. 2019. "The Secret to Mindful Travel? A walk in the woods." *Travel, National Geographic*. October 18, 2019, https://www.nationalgeographic.com/travel/article/forest-bathing-nature-walk-health/ (accessed October 27, 2022).

Koeppel, Dan. 2006. *To See Every Bird on Earth—A Father, a Son, and a Lifelong Obsession*. New York: Plume.

Tomlin, Jimmy. 2021. "Rare Spoonbill Sighting at Oak Hollow Lake Excites Local Birders." *The High Point Enterprise*. June 28, 2021. https://www.hpenews.com/news/rare-spoonbill-sighting-at-oak-hollow-lake-excites-local-birders/article_089be829-8925-5b27-8b47-63ec84695dbf.html /(accessed October 27, 2022).

Made in the USA
Columbia, SC
20 February 2023